The Dark Ages

A Captivating Guide to the Period Between the Fall of the Roman Empire and the Renaissance

© Copyright 2019

All Rights Reserved. No part of this book may be reproduced in any form without permission in writing from the author. Reviewers may quote brief passages in reviews.

Disclaimer: No part of this publication may be reproduced or transmitted in any form or by any means, mechanical or electronic, including photocopying or recording, or by any information storage and retrieval system, or transmitted by email without permission in writing from the publisher.

While all attempts have been made to verify the information provided in this publication, neither the author nor the publisher assumes any responsibility for errors, omissions or contrary interpretations of the subject matter herein.

This book is for entertainment purposes only. The views expressed are those of the author alone, and should not be taken as expert instruction or commands. The reader is responsible for his or her own actions.

Adherence to all applicable laws and regulations, including international, federal, state and local laws governing professional licensing, business practices, advertising and all other aspects of doing business in the US, Canada, UK or any other jurisdiction is the sole responsibility of the purchaser or reader.

Neither the author nor the publisher assumes any responsibility or liability whatsoever on the behalf of the purchaser or reader of these materials. Any perceived slight of any individual or organization is purely unintentional.

Free Bonus from Captivating History (Available for a Limited time)

Hi History Lovers!

Now you have a chance to join our exclusive history list so you can get your first history ebook for free as well as discounts and a potential to get more history books for free! Simply visit the link below to join.

Captivatinghistory.com/ebook

Also, make sure to follow us on Facebook, Twitter and Youtube by searching for Captivating History.

Contents

INTRODUCTION 1

CHAPTER 1 – THE MISCONCEPTION OF THE DARK AGES 5

CHAPTER 2 – THE WORLD AFTER ROME 10

CHAPTER 3 – THE RISE OF THE CHRISTIAN CHURCH 18

CHAPTER 4 – ROME CONTINUES – THE BYZANTINE EMPIRE 23

CHAPTER 5 – THE RISE OF THE CALIPHATE AND THE CONQUEST OF SPAIN 28

CHAPTER 6 – THE LOMBARD KINGDOM 35

CHAPTER 7 – CHARLEMAGNE 43

CHAPTER 8 – THE TREATY OF VERDUN AND THE RURIK DYNASTY – BEGINNINGS OF MODERN NATIONS 50

CHAPTER 9 – ALFRED THE GREAT 56

CHAPTER 10 – OTTO 1 AND THE FOUNDING OF A LOOSE FEDERATION 61

CHAPTER 11 – THE REIGN OF VENICE 69

CHAPTER 12 – THE VIKINGS 73

CHAPTER 13 – THE SECOND HALF OF THE MIDDLE AGES 80

CHAPTER 14 – THE RENAISSANCE 90

CONCLUSION 96

BIBLIOGRAPHY 101

Introduction

The Dark Ages was an interesting period of about six centuries that is largely lost to recorded history. Following the fall of Rome in 476 CE, the entire dynamic of Europe underwent a complete shift in power and culture. Under the Roman Empire, Europe was not quite as cohesive as people often think it was because many of its subjected peoples were allowed to keep their own cultures and beliefs. The important thing to the Romans was that the conquered countries of Europe submitted to Roman domination. As long as the people that the Romans were taking over agreed to be governed by Rome, their way of life was only marginally affected.

Once the city of Rome fell, though, the people who thrived in the city fled to Constantinople, the capital of the Eastern Roman Empire. Although their location changed, their way of life remained largely the same, and Constantinople became the hub for European culture for the next 1,000 years.

The rest of Europe descended into something that was not quite chaos but certainly did not have the organization that much of the continent had enjoyed under the Roman Empire. The Byzantine Empire, also known as the Eastern Roman Empire, would try to reclaim areas of Europe as part of the new Roman Empire but would largely fail. Without Rome as the central hub, there was a vacuum that many people began to try to fill. There were a couple of nearly successful attempts during the Dark Ages to unite Europe as a single entity, but no one would reach the same level of success that Rome did. The most famous attempt to reunite the continent was under Charlemagne, but he ultimately failed because there was no one strong enough to control the regions he conquered. Instead of uniting all of the regions, it ended up becoming even more broken not too long after Charlemagne's death.

While no one was able to take control of the continent under a single national banner or as part of an empire, there was one unifying element that had spread across the continent during the Roman Empire—religion. Rome had fallen, but it would rise again as the center for a belief structure that would control nearly every part of the continent. Perhaps the people could not accept a single king or nation because of their differences, but they were more than willing to accept a single religious figure. The reverence that people held for Rome continued long after the city fell, making it a logical place for the seat of the Christian Church. Over time, the figureheads would lose sight of what was important, and corruption would come to soil the reputation of the Church. By the time of Chaucer in the 14th century, this corruption would be one of the worst kept secrets. Before this period, though, there was a lot of goodwill and a sincere attempt to provide religious instruction. By the end of the 10th century, though, that desire to provide salvation to the population had already begun to be warped and twisted as the figureheads began to seek power and control over the different countries and the secular lives of the people instead of the values taught in the early days of the Church.

By 1000 CE, several cities and nations began to form and control their respective regions of the continent. Many of the nations of today had their roots in this period in time. Naturally, they would change and shift a lot over the next 1,000 years to become what they are today, but the Dark Ages saw the rise of most of the major

European nations that would eventually leave their mark on the world over the last few centuries leading to the present day. During this time, Venice also rose to a position of prominence. Their location as a port city meant that it was a hub for traders from not only Europe but the Near and Far East. Venice's power rivaled that of Rome at its height, and there would continue to be tensions between the two cities for several hundred years.

Perhaps one of the most fascinating cultures to rise and fade during this time was the Vikings. Today they are thought of in terms of cartoons, movies, gritty shows, and Norse mythology. However, the reality of the Vikings was far more varied and intellectual than most people realize, and their effect on Europe is weaved into nearly every modern nation, particularly the nations of the United Kingdom. While raiding and pillaging was a part of their culture, it was no worse or more barbaric than what the Romans did. They had a curiosity that would not be echoed by other Europeans for several hundred years. This curiosity brought them all the way across the Atlantic Ocean and saw them getting to know the native peoples there. The fact that the Vikings came, learned, and then left shows that they weren't nearly as barbaric as they are usually portrayed to be. They didn't pillage and plunder both of the new continents the way the "civilized" Europeans would toward the end of the Middle Ages and the beginning of the early modern era. Fighting was a necessity for them, but they were not trying to completely dominate and destroy other lands and cultures for the profit of their people as their curiosity was far more intense than their greed. Their fierce reputation likely comes from their success and how merciless they could be toward their enemies or the people they conquered. Considering they were a people who did not keep written records, the fact that nearly everyone knows the basics about them shows just how much their time influenced the future of Europe.

The Middle Ages is typically thought to have lasted about 1,000 years, but the Dark Ages is often considered to have ended around 1000 CE. By the time of the Renaissance, people had already become more enlightened, or at least the history was better recorded. Europe had begun to take shape into what it would eventually become, and the people were more interested in recording how that had happened. During the Dark Ages, Europe was still trying to figure out what it was and how it would survive the chaos after the fall of Rome instead of focusing on recording history. The histories recorded in Constantinople were largely specific to the time before Rome fell and the rise of the Byzantine Empire. Most of Western European history was lost to time as a result.

Chapter 1 – The Misconception of the Dark Ages

The meaning of the term Dark Ages can be disputed on several different levels. When it comes to trying to define the time that falls under this moniker, there isn't too much consensus.

For the purposes of this book, the Dark Ages will cover between the 4th century when Rome fell to the beginning of the 11th century when some of the major nations of modern-day Europe began to really take shape. Others label the period of the Dark Ages as being from the fall of Rome until the 14th century. Some people even consider the Dark Ages as being synonymous with the Middle Ages, which stretched until the Italian Renaissance.

Historians have taken to calling the Dark Ages the early Middle Ages, which is really a more accurate description. There are many things that historians debate about this time, and one of the few things that most of them can agree on is that the term Dark Ages is really a misnomer. When people discuss this time in history, they typically focus on the negative aspects, in part because that is what the term encourages people to think about. Most historians won't even use the term Dark Ages because it implies several different negative connotations, many of which are inaccurate at best and a disservice at worst.

Somewhat ironically, the term Dark Ages actually comes from Francesco Petrarca, a man better known today as Petrarch. He was a prominent scholar and poet during the 14th century (he was born in 1304 and died in 1374). To this particular Italian scholar, literature and the ideas of the time were seriously degraded compared to the literature of the Roman Empire. He thought that there were no major literary achievements that could define the culture of the Dark Ages in the same way as the Romans had done with the works of the Greeks, such as the *Iliad* and the *Odyssey*. To him, the Dark Ages meant a lack of the kind of culture that could be found in Western Europe before the Roman Empire lost control of the continent.

For people who follow Christianity, the term Dark Ages is applied because of the religious turmoil that was rife after the empire fell. Two very different thought processes about Christianity began to form, and until 1000 CE, there was a tentative peace between those two ideas. By the start of the 11th century, there was a lot of tension, but there was still only one Christian Church. This did not last for much longer, but it still held true for this time. There was also a reason for the two Christian ideologies to bring Christians together—the invasion of Muslims in Western Europe. With a common enemy, it was easier to lay aside different ideologies and band together under a single religion. Since this was a time when the differences of the two ideologies were overlooked, and people would recognize each other under the umbrella of the same religion instead of focusing on their differences, dark is really not the correct term to describe the period. If anything, it seems like a more enlightened and tolerant time, particularly compared to what was to come. The Christian Church fractured multiple times after 1000 CE, and each time, the tension would inspire more extreme reactions. The Great Schism would result in the official formation of two different churches, the Roman Catholic Church and the Greek Orthodox Church. While it was a huge scar on the religion that was supposed to be founded on mercy and understanding, it at least did not result in much bloodshed (at least not until the Crusades, which would go horribly wrong and see the sacking of Constantinople by Roman Catholics). During the early modern era, though, the rise of Protestantism would see bloodshed across all of Western Europe with Christians fighting each other over even smaller differences than the ones that caused the Great Schism. If anything, the more recent history of Christianity was actually the dark ages as the time up until 1000 CE was much more enlightened by comparison.

Some also consider this period to be dark because there is a belief that the people were more barbaric. They believe that the people roaming across Europe were cruel, cutting each other down to gain power. While this is certainly true to some extent, it is difficult to argue that it was any worse than anything that has happened since. The wars during this time were no more horrific than the Napoleonic Wars, and they pretty much had the same motivations. It could certainly be argued that the battles and wars of this time were actually less barbaric than the events of either World War.

There is one perception that is true of this time, though, and that is its lack of technological advances. The inventions and ideas that spread under the Roman Empire were largely lost. People found daily survival to be difficult, and the emerging social structures certainly did not promote maintaining that technology, let alone pushing it forward. However, much of the technology that is awe-inspiring today (such as Roman irrigation systems) really didn't exist across most of Western Europe, even the parts that were under the Roman Empire. The day-to-day life did not change that much for the majority of the people. In and around the cities, people suffered, but most of Europe didn't see too much of a change. What was lost was that push to invent. As technology and ideas declined in and around the cities, there were fewer innovative ideas. However, that does not mean that progress entirely stopped. Advances in farming saw a significant shift during the Middle Ages. By eliminating the constant fear that food would run out, people began to have more time to consider other changes and inventions.

To historians, calling this period the Dark Ages is somewhat accurate since there isn't that much known about the daily lives and events of the time. This is actually being remedied though as archeologists and scientists study findings and test items found from this period in human history. Since there was a lot of data that was lost to time, it is unlikely that the period will ever be as fully understood. However, a clearer picture is being created of how people lived and died during the Dark Ages.

Fortunately, much of the history of this time is not up for debate. Granted, there isn't nearly as much known about the lives and cultures of the people in Western Europe after the fall of Rome until 1000 CE, but many of the major events, such as the conquests of Charlemagne, were recorded and are known today.

Given the fact that the term itself stems from the desire to denote Petrarch's dissatisfaction with the way things were going, it is a term that is best forgotten instead of being perpetuated. It was essentially a part of a smear campaign against previous eras to prove that the men of Petrarch's time were becoming more enlightened by returning to the ideas and literature of the Roman Empire and ancient Greece. This is somewhat humorous as they were somewhat selective about what they returned to, as they did not start suddenly worshiping the gods and heroes of the ancient Greeks and Romans.

During the Protestant Reformation, the Dark Ages referred to the time from the fall of Rome until their present day (476 CE to the 16th century). To Protestants, Europe under the Roman Catholic Church was just as backward as anything that happened before 1000 CE. It was the Protestants who were making the continent more enlightened by discarding the control of the Catholic Church in favor of more independent thinking.

The term Dark Ages is really inaccurate in nearly all of its applications. As it is still in use, it is being adapted for this book but with the knowledge that it is a poor description of the period. In a couple hundred years, people may look back on the present day and feel that the Dark Ages is just as apt a description of our time. Thinking of the era as the early Middle Ages is both more accurate and provides a much better understanding of the timeframe of the period.

Chapter 2 – The World after Rome

The fall of Rome was like the fall of many of the other empires and civilizations before it (and many that followed it). It was never a matter of if the city would fall but rather when. Civilizations always go through periods of growth and then a slow decline. It doesn't happen all at once, and even the end of the power of Rome didn't happen overnight. The sacking of Rome wasn't the end of the Western Roman Empire because there was still an emperor for a while longer. When the city was attacked, it simply sped up the decline instead of allowing it to continue to languish and deteriorate. The fall of the city sent shockwaves across the continent, but the farther from the city that people lived, the less obvious the effects of the loss of Rome were. Some places were even happy to see the end of the Romans in their domain.

Signs of the End of Rome

One of the major signs that Rome was no longer the powerhouse that it had once been was the decay of the city and the overall maintenance of the realm that had been employed at the empire's height. The people in power were more like vultures picking apart the languishing empire than actual rulers. There were a few good leaders in the last 100 years or so, but they were in the minority. The infighting of this period mirrored that of the end of the Roman Republic a few hundred years earlier, which had ended with Julius

Caesar taking control and largely removing the senators from power. Several hundred years later, the people of Rome had forgotten the lessons of the decline of the Roman Republic, and so, they were doomed to repeat it.

As people sought to fulfill their own petty ambitions and greed, the extensive control of the empire steadily slipped away. Rome's inability to provide for the people on the outskirts of their borders would actually be the catalyst for the attacks that would be the poignant beginning of the end for ancient Rome.

There were several warning signs that should have let the Romans know that they were going down a path to destruction. Men like Nero and Caligula are still remembered today for their wild demands and their indifference toward the people they ruled over. Allowing men like that to remain in power helped to destroy the empire because it shook the people's faith in Rome. They were a symptom, though, and not the cause for the fall.

Underestimating the Enemy

The Romans suffered from the same kind of hubris that they warned others about. Believing blindly in their own invincibility, they didn't think that it would be possible for anyone to successfully attack their city. Whenever there were signs of trouble, the people in power would pull back their military to protect the core of the empire, leaving the people in the outlying territories vulnerable to attack. This was against the agreements that Rome had established with those territories when they had either negotiated control or taken it through war.

To the people in Rome, the people of these far northern regions, such as what would become the UK and northern parts of Europe, posed little to no threat because they were unsophisticated and uneducated. It seemed ridiculous to even consider them as a danger to the empire. However, this gross underestimation would be what left Rome vulnerable to the people they considered to be inferior.

In the early days, though, the Roman emperors were adept military men who had helped conquer most of the continent. Over time, the rulers became more like pampered brats who did not understand the importance of keeping their agreements with the people they ruled. Providing the necessary supplies and assistance during times of trouble would have meant less money for the rulers to use on their personal projects and whims.

However, perhaps the most critical error as a result of their ignorance was in their belief that the populations in the lands under their control were uneducated and lacked the kind of training that the people of Rome and its surrounding areas had. The reality was that many of the men who lived in those regions had served in the Roman military, fighting for the empire They were not only educated, but they were incredibly well trained in the tactics used by the Roman military. Many of the Roman officers came from these areas, some because of their awe for the Roman military's abilities and others to just serve the empire. These men were loyal to the empire and had certain expectations of what the empire would provide.

When Rome did not meet their obligations, faith in the empire began to crumble in the outer regions. This came to a head when the Huns, who had swept across western Asia and into eastern Europe, began to encroach on the Goths' territory, who lived beyond the border of the Roman Empire with other Germanic tribes. Seeking protection from the Roman Empire, the leader of the Goths sent a request to the emperor that his people be allowed to settle on Roman lands so that they would have Roman protection. Emperor Valens appeared to ignore the request because the number of Goths seeking security was more than he believed the Roman Empire could sustain. Again, the Gothic leader wrote to the emperor imploring him to allow the Goths to occupy the lands because of the imminent threat posed by the Huns. And again, the emperor did not respond.

As winter neared, the Goths knew that they were running out of time to occupy a new land and still have time to plant and harvest crops before winter fell. They began to panic, and their leader was no longer able to accept the silence from Emperor Valens. Though Valens was trying to learn more about the people seeking his protection, he should have sent some kind of response. His lack of understanding of the situation coupled with his own distance from the threat blinded him to the dangers he was making for himself and Rome by ignoring such a large population of people who had been on good terms with Rome before. Unwilling to continue to wait, the Goths settled in the territory without approval from the emperor.

The result was the Battle of Hadrianopolis (also called Adrianople) in 378 CE. The Goths vastly outnumbered the Romans, and the encounter went about as could be expected. With an estimated 10,000 to 20,000 Roman soldiers killed, Rome lost about two-thirds of their military. Emperor Valens also died during this encounter.

After having lost so spectacularly, the Romans had to allow the Goths to settle within their boundaries because they now had a whole different set of problems to contend with, starting with putting a new emperor in place. A tentative peace reigned, but tensions continued to boil under the surface.

Seeing their chance to take back their own areas, other unfriendly Germanic tribes began to chip away at the edges of the empire. More than 100 years before the time that historians consider to be the fall of Rome, the Western Roman Empire was already losing its power and lands. Rome was considerably smaller by the time it actually fell. The Battle of Hadrianopolis was just the first time that the Romans seriously underestimated their enemy.

This would be highlighted again when Rome failed to meet its obligations to the Visigoths, a western tribe of the Goths, around the end of the 3rd century. Their leader was Alaric, a man who had served as an officer in the Roman military. He was like a living bridge between his people and the empire that he had served with distinction for years. Rome had promised him that he and his people would be allowed to settle in lands in the Balkans; however, the emperor again failed to respond to the request to be allowed to settle. This nearly identical mistake was made by the Western Roman Emperor Honorius.

Instead of taking his people to settle the lands as the Goths had done, Alaric began to make additional demands of the emperor, the most notable being that the emperor grant Alaric's people Roman citizenship. This would give the Visigoths benefits that were not offered to non-Romans. The kinds of benefits they would gain included the ability to vote, inherit land, and be protected by Roman law.

Emperor Honorius finally responded with a denial of the request, and every new request was met with a denial as well. Just like Emperor Valens, Emperor Honorius was catastrophically underestimating his opponent.

Alaric had distinguished himself as a part of the Roman military, and he had brought their fighting style back to his people. He knew how to command a battlefield, and more importantly, he knew how to force his opponent to surrender. As a Christian and a leader, he was very rigid in his understanding of right and wrong, and in this case, it was clear that Rome was in the wrong. To rectify this, he was going to use what he had learned as a member of their military to force the emperor to fulfill his original promise.

It should be noted that at no time did he intend to cause the fall of Rome or to destroy the empire. He sought only to get what he and his people had been promised. Given his years of service, it was a grave mistake for Rome to try to renege on that promise. It was just a sign of how blind the emperors had become to their obligations.

Unwilling to sit and wait or to dishonor his service by claiming the lands, Alaric called his men to arms and marched them down to Rome. The emperor displayed an obscene lack of understanding of the situation by completely disregarding the large Visigothic army marching toward Rome. Or he did until they blocked all of the roads, causing trade to all but cease between Rome and the rest of the empire. Alaric used his knowledge of how to keep his troops motivated, organized, and under his control to utterly hobble Rome. While this happened, the incompetent Emperor Honorius was relaxing in his villa in Ravenna, the current capital of the Western Roman Empire, which was located outside of the city.

As they controlled the roads, Alaric's troops did not suffer during this time. They were able to trade and get supplies from the very people that they blocked from reaching the city. The people living in Rome, though, were not so fortunate. Water and food began to become scarce, significantly weakening the protection of the city. All while the emperor continued to ignore the demands for him to fulfill his promise to Alaric and his people.

Seeing no other options, Alaric and his military entered Rome in 410 CE, and they accomplished what few had accomplished before. They sacked the city of Rome. It took them only three days before they left with whatever they could take with them. The only exception was that Alaric would not allow his men to remove or harm anything from the basilicas of St. Paul and St. Peter. The 6,000 men that Emperor Honorius had finally sent didn't stand a chance against the well-armed and well-organized army of Alaric.

Although Rome would continue to have some modicum of control over the empire for about another half-century, it was merely a shadow of its former self. The last emperor, Romulus Augustulus, was only fourteen years old when he rose to his position in 475 CE, and he did not last as emperor for more than a year. He was mostly a puppet of his father, and when the Germanic warlord Odoacer killed the emperor's father in 476 CE, he offered the boy emperor retirement and then sent him away to live out the rest of his life elsewhere. Odoacer took control of the rest of the military and sent envoys to Constantinople, the capital of the Eastern Roman Empire.

This series of events was considered to be the end of the Western Roman Empire.

Coping after the Empire Crumbled

What many people don't realize is that the fall of Rome was not the end of the empire as the people of the time knew it, but just the loss of one of its major cities. Western Europe did see the Western Roman Empire crumble, but Eastern Europe and the Eastern Roman Empire continued to prosper and thrive. This is part of the reason why calling this time the Dark Ages is incredibly inaccurate—technology and civilization continued to move forward, just not in the parts of Europe that would become developed in more recent history. In what is known today as the Byzantine Empire, there was no loss of ingenuity, culture, architecture, or anything else that people associate with ancient Rome. However, the role of the Byzantine Empire is much larger than a short section can address, and there remains extensive information on that particular empire today. Chapter 4 provides an overview of how they perpetuated everything that had made Rome so influential.

Western Europe splintered, and people who still considered themselves as being Roman began taking control of their own much smaller domains. These rulers continued to use many of the same laws and principles that had been the cornerstone of the empire. Essentially what happened across Western Europe was an evolution that was unfettered from the decaying empire. People returned to the homes of their ancestors, no longer tied to an empire that had become increasingly less responsive to their needs.

The reconfiguration of the lands that had been a part of the empire naturally saw a lot of wars as different peoples tried to claim their ancestral lands, take advantage of the power vacuum, or to establish something more beneficial for their people. For these people, life changed significantly.

But for about 90% of the population though, there was no real change. Peasants and slaves did not see any real change in their daily lives. The skirmishes and battles for control clearly harmed them, but this was likely not too much different than the same skirmishes and battles that occurred during the decline of the empire. Life was not harsher or easier than it had been before the last emperor retired. For all of the beauty and progress made by Rome, it was really only a small percentage of the population that had benefited from it. The Roman elite had also been incredibly cruel to anyone who tried to upset the system that benefited this small minority of the populace, keeping the rest of the empire under their thumb. Their blind belief that things would stay the same caused the mistakes that would ultimately hurt them the most. The Germanic tribes that they had looked down on and fed to wild beasts in the Coliseum would get their revenge, leaving the elite dead or living a way of life that was vastly different than before.

The most interesting changes were in the areas outside of Rome in the places that they had the most difficulty taming. The small island of Britain that would one day be the foundation for a completely different empire was one of the first areas that Rome had left to its own devices, even before Rome fell. The regions that would one day form the major nations of continental Europe (Spain, Portugal, France, and the Holy Roman Empire) also spent the next few hundred years fighting off invaders and beginning to form the early roots for what they would eventually become.

Chapter 3 – The Rise of the Christian Church

In the beginning, Christianity was more of a sect of Judaism than a stand-alone religion. Over time, it grew in popularity and gained respect, spreading all across the Roman Empire. Initially, the people who were believers of this religion were treated with contempt, and the Romans enjoyed literally tormenting Christians to death. However, by the time Rome fell, Christianity had become a religion of its own that had drawn in people from around the continent.

The corruption of Rome by the end of the Western Roman Empire had not seen a loss of the teachings of what today is called Roman mythology. Rather, the two religions had followers who lived side by side. However, the strength of the Germanic tribes who were Christian began to attract followers from the old gods. As Rome was repeatedly defeated by members of this new religion, the worship of the old gods was abandoned.

Following the sacking of Rome and the end of the Western Roman Empire, Christianity emerged as the dominant religion, even in Constantinople. The old gods eventually drifted into obscurity and then into mythology. Christianity evolved from a religion that sought to teach salvation into a much larger, more organized, and more powerful religion. By the end of the Dark Ages, the religion was almost unrecognizable from its humble beginnings. While it had once been one of the few things that helped to unify people across the continent, it became a religion with a centralized power base that eventually became just as corrupt as the Roman Empire. During the Dark Ages, though, the religion was still finding itself and attracting followers through less violent means.

Persecution and Acceptance in Rome

Christianity began with Jesus, but his followers took up his teachings and spread them beyond Judea. Paul of Tarsus became the biggest proponent of the religion. It began as an incredibly unorganized sect that sought to save souls after death through Jesus' teachings. While Judaism was recognized by the Roman Empire, Christianity was not. Christianity was considered to be a Jewish sect though and not a formal religion at the time, so it did not receive the same protections as the root religion from which it started.

As a result, officials of the Roman Empire would occasionally persecute the followers of Christianity. Sometimes, Christians were even used in the Coliseum as entertainment as they were torn apart by wild animals. For the most part, though, the Romans tended to ignore this small sect, even as it spread across the empire. It was typically Roman policy to let the conquered regions continue with their own beliefs. The exception to this was when people would begin to directly challenge Roman authority. When this happened, the Romans would quickly act to stop them. This more laissez-faire approach to managing their territories was part of what made it so easy for Christianity to spread as far as it did in those early days.

As Christianity became a more prominent religion, the people in Rome began to take note. This soon persuaded Emperor Constantine I to issue the Edict of Milan. This edict provided legal status to a number of religions within the Roman Empire, including Christianity, in 313 CE. More than a decade later in 325 CE, the emperor introduced the Council of Nicaea. The primary purpose of this council was to establish the primary beliefs of Christianity. The end result was the Nicene Creed, which states the basic precepts and beliefs of Christianity in a concise form. Christianity was finally gaining more tangible power and organization.

Still, it did not replace the beliefs of the Romans. That did not occur until 380 CE when Emperor Theodosius I issued his Edict of Thessalonica. The form of Christianity followed by Constantine (commonly referred to as Nicene Christianity) was the form of Christianity that became the empire's official religion. All other forms of Christianity were banned, losing their protection under Emperor Theodosius. This was the first major event of persecution that was instigated by a powerful Christian figure, but it would not be the last, unfortunately.

A Sign from God

By the time Rome fell, Christianity had become a recognized and powerful religion, and it was still spreading across the continent. Many of the Germanic tribes were Christian, for example, the Goths. In Rome, however, there were still many followers of the old Roman religion with its pantheon of gods.

Once Rome ceased to be the center of its empire, people began to see its fall as a sign that the Roman gods were not as strong as the Christian god. After all, the Christian god helped the Germanic tribes win two major battles against Roman emperors. It seemed obvious that the Roman gods were not able to stand up to such a powerful god that was leading his people to victory.

With many people in Europe taking the fall of Rome as a religious sign, Christianity saw a rise in popularity and a further evolution from its teachings of forgiveness, tolerance, and pacifism. The sign that the Christian god was more powerful than other gods persuaded many people in Europe to follow the Christian teachings, giving the Christian Church even more power. With this newfound power came disagreements in how to interpret the old teachings. This eventually caused a great divide between Eastern and Western Christianity, but that did not happen until after 1000 CE.

A Melding of Beliefs

The different Christian religions across Europe tended to disagree with each other, typically claiming that they were the right religion and that other teachings were wrong or a form of heresy. However, when it came to converting others to their religion, they often worked together with other religions. Many of the Christian holidays (if not all of them) are actually based on the celebrations or observances of other religions.

Perhaps the best well-known of these holidays is Easter, which was actually a pagan celebration of spring and the renewal of the world in new life. This festival began with the Saxons to celebrate their goddess Eostra, who gave humanity spring every year. One of the reasons that it was easy to start to transform this celebration into a Christian holiday is that the spring celebration began around the time of the Jewish Passover holiday, a holiday that was still being observed by Christians. The name for Passover celebrates the Jewish being liberated from slavery in ancient Egypt, and the name comes from the "passing over" of the homes in ancient Egypt that belonged to the Jewish slaves. Any home that was not marked was said to have been visited by the holy spirit who killed the eldest son.

The correlation between the renewal of life had obvious parallels. However, Christianity needed something more specific to their religion instead of being tied to Judaism. Instead of equating the holiday with Passover, they chose to correlate it to the death and resurrection of Jesus. This had even more obvious connections to the theme of renewal, and it helped to persuade the pagans to convert to Christianity through repurposing one of the main pagan holidays.

This was a method that the Christian Church would use during most of the early Middle Ages. Since they would adapt holidays to meet the needs of their religion and then spread the holiday across the continent, it does make it difficult to know exactly when the historical events of the religion actually occurred. For example, for the first few hundred years, Christians did not celebrate the birth of Jesus because it was considered wrong to recognize the birth of a martyr as a holiday. It was only in 221 CE (a little less than 200 years after his death) that Christians began to acknowledge the holiday, and they set it for December 25th. This coincided with the Roman celebration of the winter solstice and likely did not reflect the actual date of the birth of Jesus.

Nicaean Christianity also did not abandon the teachings, culture, or beliefs of the Roman Empire. As the Christian Church did with many of the religions and cultures that it encountered across Europe, it took different aspects of the Roman Empire and adapted it to fit into the teachings of Christianity. Looking at the Roman Catholic Church, many of the beliefs and structures came from the ancient empire. The fact that the Church's services continued to be delivered in Latin until the end of the 20th century shows just how much influence the empire had on the religion. Even the name of the head of the Church, the pope, is derived from the official title of the high priest of the Roman pantheon. The term *Pontifex Maximus* was used to denote the head of the Christian church, with one of his official titles being Supreme Pontiff.

Chapter 4 – Rome Continues – The Byzantine Empire

As mentioned in Chapter 2, the sacking of Rome and the removal of the last Roman emperor was not viewed as an end to the Roman Empire. There were two major cities that ruled the Roman Empire, each of which had its own ruler. Rome was certainly where the empire started, but it had become so large during its peak that it required a second city and ruler to manage the far eastern side of the empire.

The idea that everything was lost when Rome fell is obviously wrong as much of the traditions, literature, and even its mythology is well known today. Much of the information about the Roman Empire was preserved by the people in Constantinople, ensuring that the events, people, and the culture were preserved long after the fall of the illustrious city.

The effects of the fall were felt all the way to the east as well. The two cities may have been ruled separately, but they still worked together. Without Rome, Constantinople had to deal with issues like debt and protection without the strength of the Roman military. They did have their own military, social structure, and laws, but there had always been a level of security to their western side that was lost without their sister city.

The Need for a Second Ruler

Most people consider Rome to be the center of the Roman Empire. That is where the empire began, but perpetual expansion made it too difficult for a single city to manage every territory within the empire. The split occurred in 285 CE under Emperor Diocletian. By dividing control with the city to the east, governing the two vastly different areas became more manageable. Rome was the capital for the western portion of the empire, and Byzantium was the capital for the eastern side. The eastern capital would later be renamed Constantinople.

The two halves of this extensive empire continued to prosper with neither half being considered more vital or in control than the other. Things began to change about 100 years later under Emperor Theodosius, the same emperor who banned all versions of Christianity that didn't conform to Nicene Christianity. Between 379 and 395 CE, the emperor of the west became more tyrannical than previous emperors, and his zeal for Christianity proved to be detrimental to the tolerance that was a part of the Christian religion before his reign. Theodosius wanted to not only rid the empire of pagan beliefs but to force all Christians to conform to what he believed to be the right set of beliefs. This caused a rift between the two halves of the empire, splitting them into the Western Roman Empire and the Byzantine Empire. However, these terms were created after the fall of the empire, and people back then would have considered themselves a part of the Roman Empire, regardless of which empire they lived in.

The division had been growing for some time, so the different ideologies were always destined to divide the two halves of the empire further. Some of the emperors in the eastern half never even traveled to Rome, highlighting the fact that they were their own source of power.

Over time, Rome continued to focus on religious control and power. Their lack of focus on maintaining their portion of the empire and neglecting to uphold their agreements with the peoples of their subject territories resulted in their demise. The region under the protection and control of Constantinople did not suffer the same fate. They were more lenient, and their policies helped them grow to be more prestigious and powerful as Rome declined. It would prove to be incredibly fortunate that the two halves had split. As Rome declined, the people under Byzantine rule continued the traditions and culture that had gotten their start in Rome.

The Effects of the Fall of Rome

Although it was separate from Rome, Constantinople and the eastern half of the empire still felt the effects of the loss of what was once the most powerful city in Europe. From a practical standpoint, the Germanic tribes that had chipped away and ultimately sacked Rome were now a threat to the western border of the Eastern Roman Empire.

The capital itself was less susceptible to attacks because of its location. Because it overlooked a strait, trying to invade the city would prove to be every bit as difficult to achieve as it had been to sack Rome. And it took nearly as long for the inevitable to happen in Constantinople. The Germanic tribes did pose a threat to the Byzantine Empire, but with a much smaller frontier, the risks to the eastern half were not nearly as great as it had been for Rome. This would change over time as the Byzantine Empire spread, but in the years immediately following the fall of Rome, the eastern capital and the lands under its domain were secure.

There had always been a separation of ideology between the two powerful cities, and once the eastern half became the only surviving half, it continued to move away from the Latin roots of Rome as it favored the Greek traditions. While it didn't completely discard the culture of Rome, the Eastern Roman Empire shifted more toward following the Greek traditions. Despite this, the Byzantine Empire did continue some of the traditions of Rome that had made it so vast and powerful. The leaders of Constantinople exercised strong control over the administrative aspects of governing its people, managing to keep the city and its lands stable during such an uncertain time. They also had a firm grasp on the economic problems and methods to minimize the loss of its other half. Being aware of how important their military was, the administrators and emperor of the Byzantine Empire made sure that their military remained strong and was well funded. They managed their resources much more efficiently than Rome had during its decline.

Building a New Empire

Even without Rome, the eastern half of the empire blossomed. There were no emperors with whom they had to coordinate, compromise, or argue about how the city and its lands should be run. Having secured their borders by growing their military, they soon became an incredibly influential player in Europe, the Near East, and Northern Africa. However, they never managed to reclaim much of continental Europe.

There were many notable rulers of the new empire as well. Men like Emperor Justinian managed to help expand the empire, stretching its reach well beyond the boundaries that it held following Rome's fall. Unlike the Western Roman Empire in its waning years, the people in the Eastern Roman Empire had opportunities that went well beyond their station. Emperor Justinian himself actually came from a low station in life, and his wife, Empress Theodora, was a courtesan prior to her marriage to Justinian. By helping the people in lower stations to rise, the empire began to thrive because these people better understood the plight of the lower classes. The laws and beliefs were based on a more humanitarian and tolerant foundation for much of the Byzantine Empire. This would, of course, change later as it began to rot just as Rome had done. However, the early days after the fall of Rome both perpetuated the culture of Rome while establishing its own culture. For instance, some of the most impressive buildings designed and built over the next 1,000 years were made in Constantinople. Unlike the large cathedrals and structures that began to crop up all across Western Europe, the architecture of the Byzantine Empire was closer to the Roman traditions.

In the waning years of the Byzantine Empire, the people who were able to fled west as the city was attacked, and the remainder of the empire fell to the Ottoman Empire. As they left the city that had kept the legacy of Rome safe, the people brought what they could of that legacy. It is not a coincidence that the Italian Renaissance began around the end of the Byzantine Empire. Western Europe was by no means the uneducated, barbaric place that it is often portrayed as being today during the Dark Ages, but they did not have the same connection to the Roman Empire that the people of Constantinople had. The ideas and beliefs that were lost in Western Europe were restored and relearned as the people of Constantinople returned to Rome and Italy. It was the melding of the old and new ideas that helped to bring about the changes that would explode at the beginning of the modern era and permanently change the landscape of Europe.

Chapter 5 – The Rise of the Caliphate and the Conquest of Spain

The term caliphate refers to the dual political and religious state under Muslim laws. Today, it also refers to a Muslim community, though that was not true in the early days of their conquest across the Middle East, Northern Africa, and Southern Europe. The leader of a caliphate is called a caliph, which is similar in meaning to the term king or emperor. The spread of Islam began soon after the first caliph was designated and ended in 1258 CE when the Mongols entered and sacked Baghdad.

During the height of the caliphate, the religion of Islam was adopted and spread to the areas under the caliph's control, although the general population was not required to be Muslim in the early days. Most of North Africa and southeastern Asia were included in the regions that were Islamic, and many of the regions still practice the religion today.

The Caliphate Empire tried to extend into Europe, but it soon found that they were no match for the Germanic tribes that had adopted the military tactics of the Roman Empire. It was one of the few places where they were not either easily victorious or indifferently acknowledged, and they decided to continue their conquest in other regions instead of pressing farther north into Europe.

The Beginnings of a New Empire

As Christianity continued to evolve and change across Europe, a new religion was forming under the prophet Muhammad. He held religious and political power over those who followed him, but his death posed a unique problem to the religion that formed around his teachings. As the "Seal of the Prophets," those who followed Muhammad believed that he was the last prophet who would be on Earth—there would be no other prophets after him. This gave his teachings more weight than the teachings of previous prophets from the region (primarily Jewish and Christian prophets). Just like the Christians believed that the words of Jesus were the most important message to follow (more than the words of previous prophets), Muhammad's teachings were the final word and superseded the words of all other prophets.

Muhammad died in 632 CE, leaving his followers without an obvious leader. Nor did he leave any instructions on how he would be succeeded as the religious leader. However, his followers were organized, and they quickly chose one of Muhammad's fathers-in-law, Abu Bakr. Though he was not a prophet, he served as the new spiritual and political leader of Islam. Abu Bakr was selected because it was believed that he would have a better understanding of the religion started by his son-in-law and how best to implement his teachings and govern Muhammad's followers.

Over time, there was some debate about how the new caliph should be chosen, with a leaning toward descendants of the prophet or those who were in some way related to him. This eventually come to be a divisive aspect in the religion that is still felt today.

The first four caliphs were either related to the prophet or were his close companions. When Umar ibn al Khattab rose to power after the death of Abu Bakr, he wanted to spread the religion and his control over a larger area. This was the beginning of a conquest that turned this small sect into the major religion of an enormous empire. He would be the caliph from 634 to 644 CE.

Initially, the focus was on gaining control over the small tribes around them. This proved to be difficult as their army was not nearly as organized or proficient in 634, but the new caliph worked to create a military system that would be effective against the surrounding small tribes. His success began the spread of his control to the surrounding areas, and then his control started to reach toward the east and north to the Sasanian (Persian) and Byzantine Empires, respectively.

They were successful for several decades, even attacking Constantinople several times, though never successfully bringing down the capital of the Byzantine Empire. They found more success against the Sasanian Empire, eventually dissolving their culture and government and establishing the caliphate in the region.

Some point to the weakened state of the Sasanian Empire and the lack of internal structures around the areas that the new empire incorporated. There is certainly some truth to this, as many of the people in the regions that fell under the caliph's control were indifferent to the new leader. Years of strife and terrible rulers had left the people in many of these regions in difficult environments. However, with the passage of time, the empire's military became both effective and impressive. They successfully defeated the Byzantine Empire in several battles and rarely lost in their wars for conquest.

As they extended the empire, the Muslims also pushed the boundaries in science and math. The numbers used for science and math today are Arabic numerals, and education was offered across the Islamic empire. The stagnation of these kinds of interests in Europe was in stark contrast to how the Muslims strove to better the lives of the people under them. They valued education and learning because they understood the value of having people who were able to think and innovate.

Their biggest defeat came when they entered Europe and tried to extend their rule over the Germanic tribes who were still trying to figure out their own borders. If the developing areas and nations of Europe had proved anything up to this point, it was that they were more than willing to ally with each other to defeat outsiders. This willingness to ignore their differences made the Germanic tribes that applied the old Roman tactics against their enemies an incredibly formidable foe. And it was something that the Islamic commander and his men did not anticipate.

Initial Success and the First Resistance

Having experienced repeated success all across Northern Africa, the Muslim army turned to the Strait of Gibraltar to continue their expansion to the north. They made their way largely unchallenged across what would one day become Spain between 711 to 713 CE. Like many of the other places that they conquered, the Muslim military and government did not force the people to follow the religion of Islam. Instead, they took a similar approach used by Rome centuries earlier, allowing cultures and religions of their conquered territories to continue largely as they had prior to the conquest. Local governments were established under a Muslim governance, and the regions followed the financial systems established under the caliph. Over time, this approach proved to be far more effective than forcing conversion to their religion (as would be seen later in Europe when the many Christian Churches, such as the Catholic Church and Anglican Church, killed anyone who did not convert). This tolerance of other religions showed that the Muslim rulers were not only understanding of their differences but that they wanted life to improve in ways that suited the places they conquered.

They also adopted the tactics and weaponry of the areas they conquered. By the time the Muslim army spread across Spain, they had already become skilled at incorporating the techniques of Central Asia in their warfare. This proved to be instrumental in their successful conquests, and they were seldom up against people who could combat this approach.

It was only when they began to try to stretch beyond Spain and farther into Europe that the Muslim army met an opponent that they vastly underestimated. Perhaps they were expecting the same kind of weak political and military systems that could be quickly incorporated into their own. As they continued to push westward, it appeared that they would have some level of success as they encountered Duke Odo of France, who sought to form an alliance with them against the Franks who followed Charles Martel, also known as Charles the Hammer. Odo had hoped to secure his lands from the encroaching Franks through an alliance with a more powerful group, but his hopes were quickly dispelled when a new emir (ruler) rose to power after a civil war broke out across the Muslim territories. Abdul al-Rahman did not want an alliance; he wanted to continue to expand the empire. Marching his men northward, he began to enter into parts of modern-day France. The only victory that Odo found against this new enemy was during the Battle of Toulouse in 721 CE. However, the Muslims were able to take control over most of Aquitaine and Bordeaux.

Odo was now faced with the reality that the only way to stop these new invaders was to turn to the Franks and Charles Martel. In return for helping Odo, Charles required his agreement to be subject to the Franks. Knowing that he didn't have any other options, Odo agreed and then went to face the Muslims who were continuing their conquest farther into Odo's domain. When the Muslims defeated him at the Battle of the River Garonne in 732, Martel marched south to meet the advancing army. Martel was determined to choose the ground where he would begin the next battle, the Battle of Tours.

Some historians speculate that the series of events that came next demonstrated a sense of overconfidence or complacency by Abdul-al-Rahman. Perhaps believing in his own superiority after defeating Odo, he thought that conquering the remnants of the Roman Empire would be just as easy. Whatever the case, when he finally faced Martel, the Muslim commander was not ready to fight someone who had spent a lot of time studying the military tactics of the Roman Empire and Alexander the Great and then perfecting those tactics.

Having chosen where he would fight, Martel then had his men form a tight defensive formation on high ground, giving them a significant advantage over the Muslim army. Initially, Abdul al-Rahman took his time studying the Franks, with a few skirmishes breaking out over the course of several days. With the promise of wealth waiting for him in Tours, the commander decided to make a full-frontal assault against the well-positioned Franks. This played right into what Martel wanted as the uphill battle tired their horses, and it was far more difficult to penetrate the tight formation of the Franks.

Then word began to spread among the Muslim forces that some of the Franks had begun to attack their flank, taking some of the treasure the Muslims had seized as they marched north. Hearing this, the cavalry immediately turned to stop the Franks from taking their treasure that had been left behind in the tents. The rest of the military took this as a sign of retreat, and they quickly followed their cavalry. When Abdul al-Rahman tried to get them to turn around, he realized that he was vastly outnumbered by the Franks. The Franks quickly took advantage of the situation, killing the commander and sowing more chaos among his military. It is estimated that the Muslims lost about 10,000 of their soldiers during the battle as opposed to the 1,000 to 1,500 Franks who perished. Martel's strategy clearly went well beyond anything that the Muslims could have expected, making their underestimation of the enemy a grave error that cost them far more than they were willing to risk again.

This unexpected turn of events did not persuade the Muslims to leave the continent, but it did mark an end to their desire to expand farther into these particular Christian lands. The Battle of Tours gained Martel a reputation that he would use to extend his kingdom. The Muslims, on the other hand, remained entrenched in the territories they had already taken in southern France and Spain. A couple more campaigns were hazarded in 736 and 739 CE, but the results of the forays quickly reminded any ambitious commanders why moving north was not advisable. With so many territories already under the caliph's control, it was decided that trying to extend farther north against such strong opposition was unjustified. It simply wasn't worth the effort, particularly as other problems began to arise in the rest of the empire.

With the passing of time, the empire began to decay, and the caliphs focused on all the wrong things, just like with almost every other empire that fell apart. The Islamic territory began to shrink as they failed to maintain the military in a way that allowed them to keep control of their extensive lands. The people who lived under them grew discontented with the overtaxation and lack of benefits, just like the people in Rome, the Byzantine Empire, and almost every other civilization had experienced. The welcome changes that the Muslims had introduced gave way to the same kind of self-serving leaders who sought personal gain instead of the betterment of their people. The Middle Ages were just as rife with this repeated pattern as numerous empires fell victim to failing to pay attention to history and repeating the same mistakes that had ended nearly every previous empire.

Chapter 6 – The Lombard Kingdom

The Lombards were a particularly interesting Germanic tribe. Originating in the area around Scandinavia, they eventually migrated all the way down to Italy where they ruled for over 200 years. It was a very uneven rule that saw many weak and ineffective kings and a nobility that often-sought self-interest over the interest of the kingdom. A handful of leaders did expand this kingdom to become something much bigger than their humble beginnings would suggest was possible.

However, their unlucky streak of bad rulers caused a similar decline to the one seen in Rome. Infighting and a lack of skills in governing would see the Lombards offending the mighty Frankish Kingdom. If there was one thing that the Lombards did well, though, it was conforming and adapting to their new environment and rule. They may not have kept their kingdom viable for long, but they were easily incorporated into the kingdom that followed after theirs fell.

The Great Migration

There were many different Germanic tribes, and not all of them were conquered by the Romans. For roughly 100 years (376 to 476 CE), these tribes began to move and settle in new regions. While the dates are debatable, many historians cite the relocation and migration of the Goths in 376 CE as the first major event of the Great Migration. When the Goths crossed the river Danube into Roman territory, it resulted in the Roman military attacking them. The Goths had been trying to get approval from Rome to make the move, and when their request was completely ignored, they made the move anyway to escape the Huns who were encroaching on their lands. The Battle of Hadrianopolis proved that Rome was not nearly as powerful or mighty as it had once been.

Other tribes saw the success of the Goths, and many of them decided to risk the move too. With proof that Rome could be beaten, coupled with the nearly undefeated Huns on their other side, some of the Germanic tribes decided to take their chances with the Romans.

The movements of the Winnili, the ancestors of the Lombards, is shrouded in myth, making it difficult to know much more than that they had their origins in southern Scandinavia. Over the years, they became more nomadic, and their movements caused them to encounter a number of the major Germanic tribes, such as the Vandals and Saxons.

By the 1st century CE, they were living a relatively peaceful life as a part of the Suebi people. Sporadic battles occurred with the Celtic and Germanic tribes, but for the most part, the Lombards focused on agriculture over conquest. That would change around the time of the Great Migration.

Like many other Germanic tribes, the Lombards sought a place that was safer from the Hunnic threat, and so, they settled in an area just north of the Danube region. Their leader during this time was Lamissio, who was part of what is best described as a royal dynasty. He had proven himself to be a great leader prior to the migration when he rallied his men to attack the Bulgarians to help rescue a princess who the Bulgarians had kidnapped. The Lombards knew that Lamissio was not a coward, so when the threat posed by the Huns became serious, his people knew that their leader was working in their best interest. They prospered in their new lands and became a dominant force over the next century.

A Losing War and a New Kingdom

By the middle of the 6th century, the Lombards needed a new leader, and Audoin rose to power. Unlike previous leaders, Audoin took a greater interest in developing a more impressive and organized military system. Using the systems of other successful tribes around them, Audoin established a military that was based on kinship. At the top of each unit was a member of the nobility, such as a duke or a count, and the people under them were largely related to the leader. This was meant to provide a better connection and sense of comradery between the soldiers and their leader.

Audoin was able to test his new military system during a twenty-year long conflict with the Gepids, a tribe that was related to the Goths. It was his son, Alboin, who finally ended the exhaustive war by making an alliance with the Avars. They were a neighboring tribe of the Gepids, giving Alboin some support and creating another front against the Gepids. In 567 CE, Alboin, his men, and their allies killed Cunimund, the last king of the Gepids, and some sources say Alboin turned the king's skull into a goblet.

Following that victory, the Avars expected Alboin to honor their agreement which had said that all of Cunimund's land would become lands of the Avars. This soon proved to be a grave mistake on the part of Alboin because the Avars were far more controlling than the Gepids had been. The only real benefit that the Lombards gained was the marriage of Cunimund's daughter, Rosamund, to Alboin, a marriage that was forced on her as the daughter of the leader of the losing side. Seeing that they had come out worse after their twenty-year effort, Alboin knew that even the marriage alliance to the Gepids did not make his people strong enough to face the now dominant Avars. Instead of instigating another protracted war with no guarantee of success, Alboin decided that it was time for his people to leave the area. Since a number of his military had served in northern Italy, the recommendation was made to go there for their resettlement. The men remembered the region as being very green and fertile, which should have made it ideal for reestablishing their agrarian lifestyle.

Alboin and his military had greatly benefited from the years of war and service to other tribes and the remains of the Roman Empire. As they progressed across northern Italy, the Lombards were able to easily take control of many of the cities in their wake. To be fair, there wasn't much resistance against them. The only exception to this was Pavia where the Lombards spent three years fighting before they finally were victorious. Their march and subjection of Italian territories were over by 572 CE, and they had nearly all of Italy under their control. Alboin broke up the vast stretch of his new lands into 36 duchies, or territories, with a duke to rule over each of them. Each of these dukes was subject to Alboin and had to report to him directly on the status of their duchy. Alboin took up residence in Verona and began to focus his attention on keeping these new areas secure from the Franks to the west and the Byzantine Empire to the east. His dukes were left to manage their duchies, and, as could be expected, some were far more adept at it than others. There was a disparate level of success across the Lombard kingdom, creating a more divisive atmosphere across the kingdom than the unity that the shared heritage should have enjoyed.

With his attention elsewhere and his dukes more concerned with helping their respective regions to prosper, no one was looking out for the kingdom as a whole. This created a vulnerability that none of them had anticipated and one that had been a long time coming as Rosamund had never accepted Alboin as her husband or ruler. He had caused the death of her father and forced her to wed him, the man who had made a wine goblet from her father's skull. She began to help plot her husband's assassination, and she succeeded in 572 CE. Left without a primary figure to lead the Lombard Kingdom, the already fractured kingdom began to show the major cracks that were characteristic of the type of governance that controlled it.

Alboin's Fears Realized

Like many of the other Germanic tribes, the Lombards were Christian. However, they were Arian Christians, one of the heretical forms of Christianity according to the Council of Nicaea. The Arian Christians followed the teachings of Arius of Alexandria, and they did not believe in the Holy Trinity that was made a part of orthodox Christianity during the council. (One of the best examples of an Arian Christian religion today is the Jehovah's Witnesses.) This was yet another difference between the Lombards and the peoples of the surrounding areas, which put them at religious odds with the Franks and the Byzantine Empire.

The Byzantine Empire had another reason to attack the kingdom, though. Following the death of Theodoric, the Great in 526 CE, the eastern empire sought to reclaim the area that had once been the center for the Roman Empire. The attempt was costly, both in terms of money and resources. Lasting nearly thirty years (from 526 to 555 CE), there were only a few periods of time when the Byzantine Empire was not engaged in fighting the Ostrogoths who had taken over Italy. During this time, they actually allied with the Lombards to help reclaim the lands. When the Lombards decided to set up their own kingdom in the region that the Byzantine Empire had spent so much effort to reclaim, the Byzantine Empire acted quickly to counter the Lombards. The Exarchate at Ravenna was created by Emperor Maurice to reclaim the lands. Unfortunately for the Byzantine Empire, the people in the region had no interest in fighting the Lombards because they were all too familiar with the way they would be treated under the empire. The Exarchate was unable to raise the kind of force that was required to defeat the Lombards, making the endeavor almost entirely wasted.

After Alboin's death, the dukes focused on their petty squabbles for several years. However, with the formation of the Exarchate in 582 CE, they finally had a reason to work together. To address the threat, they chose a new king named Authari in 584 CE. Later that year, he defeated the forces that the Byzantine Empire had sent to attack the Lombards. This victory was short-lived as Authari would lose ground and lands the following year to the Byzantine Empire.

Authari turned to the hope of forging an alliance with the Franks to the west of Italy. Marriage negotiations began with King Childebert II for his daughter's hand. When those negotiations failed, the Frankish king gave his daughter away to one of the Visigothic kings instead. Although the Franks and the Byzantine Empire had long been enemies of each other, they formed a tentative alliance to remove the Lombards from Italy. In 590 CE, a full invasion of Italy began. The Franks proved to be even more menacing than the empire (though they were positioned directly west of Italy while the Byzantine Empire was considerably farther east) as they began to take control over major Italian cities.

Hoping that he could gain some allies, Authari married the daughter of one of the Bavarian dukes. However, he never saw the help he was trying to gain because he died in 590 CE. One of his cousins, Agilulf, soon took over the leadership position. After marrying Authari's widow, Agilulf tried to make peace with the Franks, and he was successful. Without the Franks invading to their west, Agilulf was able to strengthen the borders of the Lombard kingdom so that they were not vulnerable to the empire's efforts to reclaim Italy. His next major task was to reduce the amount of power each of the dukes had, consolidating control of the country under the king.

The Byzantine Empire soon dropped their quest to reclaim Italy as they were being attacked by the Avars and Slavs to their west and the Persians to their south. Their military was already spread too thin, and they did not have the necessary resources to recapture and control Italy.

So, without any major enemies, the Lombard Kingdom began to prosper and thrive in the ensuing peace. Despite the fact that the Lombards were Arian Christians and most of the original Italian population were Trinitarian (one of the major religions that would help form Roman Catholicism after the Great Schism), they were able to keep a comfortable peace. Religious ideologies were less divisive than what both peoples had already experienced, and the Lombards had repeatedly proven that they were better able to handle peace than war. The Italians had seen a number of conquerors come through and implement laws and taxes that were far more harmful to their existence than the differences between their religion and that of the Lombards. It was an incredibly unique peace that helped to shape Italy because while the Italians and Lombards worked together despite their religious differences, other territories were tearing each other apart because of it. Agilulf was also a shrewd tactician when it came to politics, and he agreed to have his children baptized into the Italian religion instead of his own.

This peace saw changes in the Lombards as well. They began to adopt a lifestyle that was more similar to the Italians instead of keeping their Germanic heritage. From their clothing to their weapons, the Lombards became more like the Romans prior to the fall of the Western Roman Empire, even going so far as to give their children Roman names. Although they had not taken over all of modern-day Italy, the Lombards controlled all of the north and middle of the region. The Byzantine Empire only retained control over the southern portion and Rome. Over time, the Lombards began to claim most of the rest of Italy, though they never managed to take Rome and some of the smaller southern provinces that were controlled by the Byzantine Empire.

Repeating History

While most of the Lombard Kingdom experienced peace and growth, the position of king began to change hands far too rapidly. Agilulf died in 616 CE and was succeeded by his wife until his son came of age. The new king continued his father's tolerance, which upset his brother-in-law, who then deposed him. This new king died in 636 CE and was succeeded by Rothari. It was during his reign that the Lombard Kingdom was finally expanded, removing most of the strongholds of the Byzantine Empire. His son took over the throne after Rothari's death, but he did not last long as his enemies assassinated him soon after his rise to power.

This focus on control proved to be just as telling about the future of the Lombard Kingdom as it had been about every other civilization before it, including Rome. After the death of the last king, the kingdom was divided into Milan and Pavia. These two sides fought not only each other for control, but they fought the Slavic tribes that continued to strike at their borders. One last great king would emerge in King Liutprand in 712 CE. During his reign, the kingdom expanded, and a new alliance was formed with the Franks. The Lombard Kingdom was able to experience peace and prosperity one more time under his reign, which ended in 744 CE. He was followed by ineffective rulers who focused on personal gain over the stability and security of the kingdom.

Then King Desiderius pushed the Byzantine Empire out of Italy during the early part of the 770s, but he quickly lost control of the Lombard Kingdom by threatening Pope Hadrian I. This earned him the ire of Charlemagne, who broke the alliance that had been forged under Liutprand. Desiderius did not stand a chance, and in 774 CE, he was soundly defeated by the legendary Charlemagne, ending the rule of the Lombards over Italy. Some of the effective dukes did manage to keep control over their small territories, but there was no longer a central government or primary ruler. Instead, they became a part of the Frankish Kingdom.

Chapter 7 – Charlemagne

One of the most well-known names to come out of the early Middle Ages was that of Charlemagne. Even if you don't know exactly what he did, you are probably well aware of his military prowess and that he conquered a considerable portion of Europe. Of course, the Byzantine Empire still kept much of the Roman Empire alive, but the western portion of the empire was divided into so many small kingdoms, territories, lands, and duchies that it seemed almost impossible that they would ever be brought back into a single fold.

Despite how impossible a task it seemed, Charlemagne was able to not only take control of the region of his people but to conquer surroundings areas that had become the territories of other Germanic tribes. His ability to attract followers and lead his people to victory became legendary. And for a brief moment, it seemed like he might even be able to accomplish what no one thought would ever be possible again—a restoration of an empire that would rival that of Rome.

Unfortunately, that glimmer of hope died with Charlemagne. His military prowess and inspirational leadership could not be matched by anyone who succeeded him, and the empire that he had begun to construct quickly fell apart without him.

The World into Which a Leader Was Born

Without a strong city to keep the lands united, Western Europe became little more than a bunch of warring tribes and states (at least at first glance). The truth was that not that much actually changed after the fall of Rome. Some places continued to use Roman money, and many areas continued to enforce the same laws; however, they did practice their own cultures and celebrated their own versions of Christianity or their pagan religions.

People who had been in power under the Western Roman Empire saw the breakdown of the empire as the opportunity they needed to gain the power they could never have had if Rome had not fallen. Instead of trying to find common ground, they fought to place regions under their control. Other places that had been a part of the empire saw it as a chance to return to the way things used to be, particularly the Germanic tribes that had fought against the Romans. Some of the conquered communities had never fully acclimated to the Roman way of life, and the transition back to the way things had been was far easier than trying to perpetuate a culture that they didn't want to control them.

As the former Western Roman Empire continued to fracture and splinter into different territories and kingdoms, many of the innovations and progress that had been made by the Romans began to deteriorate. Many of the regions that were far removed from Rome didn't see much change since they had not changed a great deal under Roman rule, but the closer to Rome a location was, the more they had to lose. Innovations like roads were no longer maintained, and for places near Rome, the irrigation systems began to falter and collapse. There weren't many engineers or mechanics who could repair them because people were now focused on struggling to survive instead of filling their former well-defined roles in society. It didn't help that many well-educated people fled to Constantinople, leaving no one behind with the knowledge and experience to make the necessary repairs. These structures actually had a head start in deteriorating because the later emperors tended to ignore the roads and water systems because they were too expensive to maintain. Without a central source to fund and monitor these advances, the technology was lost for centuries.

The lack of a central government also meant that the Germanic peoples who had once resided on the boundaries of the empire were now free to settle wherever they wanted to. They had begun to move into the territories under Roman control during the Great Migration, so that trend simply continued after Rome fell. The Byzantine Empire attempted to restore parts of the old empire into itself, but it was met with only a marginal victory over the Germanic tribes that continued to move farther south. They largely left the Germanic tribes to settle as they wanted because they didn't pose much of a problem to the Byzantine Empire.

This was true until the middle of the 8th century when a new leader emerged.

The Birth and Rise of a New Emperor

Charlemagne was not born into a situation that would suggest anything about what his future would be like. Although his father was King Pepin the Short, the throne that was to become Charlemagne's, if he survived to adulthood, was not a major kingdom as Pepin ruled over the Franks, who lived in what is now Belgium. Pepin celebrated the birth of Charlemagne, his first son, in 742 CE. When Pepin died in 768 CE, Charlemagne was 24 years old. He and his brother, Carloman I, were supposed to have a joint rule over the people, but that plan was shattered in 771 CE when Charlemagne's brother suddenly died.

Charlemagne had taken an interest in the military at an early age and proven himself to be an expert tactician and leader. It did not take him long to apply his knowledge and skills to expand Frankish control. One of the first major kingdoms that Charlemagne went up against was the Saxons. The Saxons, who looked down on Christians and were cruel to those that resided within their realm, were a threat that Christian Charlemagne simply could not afford to ignore. A year after the death of his brother, Charlemagne led a campaign into Saxon territories. The end result was the complete control over the former Saxon territories and the forced conversion of the Saxons to the religion that they hated so much.

Having tasted success against a formidable opponent, Charlemagne appeared to feel destined to push his control into other regions. Turning south, he took control of Italy. In 778 CE, he led an army into Spain and began to drive the Muslims out of Europe. Within twelve years, he was able to unite a large swath of Europe under Frankish rule. There were no opponents who could withstand his assaults, but over time, many didn't have any interest in displacing him.

The Roman rebellion of 800 CE saw Pope Leo III's life being put into danger. Knowing that Charlemagne was a practicing Christian, the pope requested his assistance to quell the rebellion. The problem had started with the death of Pope Adrian I. One of his relatives, Paschal, felt that he should have become the next pope, ignoring the fact that the position is not hereditary. When someone else was named to take over the head of the Church, he rallied people to help him assassinate the new pope, Pope Leo III. Paschal and his followers attacked the new pope during a procession and scattered the crowd that had come to interact with him. They savagely maimed the pope by trying to cut out his tongue and stabbing his eyes. Although he was critically injured, Leo was not killed during this first attempt, nor he was killed during a second attempt by Paschal's accomplices when the attackers realized that the pope had fled to a chapel and was very much alive.

Forced to leave the city, Leo sought the assistance of Charlemagne to restore him to his position in Rome as the head of the Church. Charlemagne obliged and escorted the pope back into the city. Once the pope was within the walls of Rome, the assailants began to verbally attack the pope, accusing him of anything that came to mind. When the discussion proved to go nowhere, Charlemagne passed judgment and called for the deaths of the conspirators. The pope negated this decision and instead offered mercy to those who had harmed him. The people who had participated in the attack were exiled instead.

Despite undoing Charlemagne's decision, the pope was grateful for his assistance. What happened next was what caused the Byzantine Empire to take a greater interest in what was going on in Western Europe. For the first time since the fall of Rome, an emperor was crowned. Pope Leo offered the title and a ceremony to Charlemagne as a way to thank the Frank for his help. This was done without consulting or even informing the Byzantine emperor. The pope's actions set an incredibly dangerous precedent: the ability to crown a new emperor based on his own decisions with no input from anyone else. This was a kind of power that no one in Western Europe had tried to claim before, and it was made with no basis in tradition or law. Western Europe was made up of many types of Christians, and the pope did not have authority over many of them. Yet he was now apparently claiming the right to select emperors over regions that were not his, making them now united under Charlemagne.

Charlemagne maintained a strong relationship with Pope Leo III, and perhaps it comes as no surprise that after Charlemagne died, Leo's position was once again threatened. Those who wanted to see the pope removed from power knew that he no longer had any protection because of the power vacuum created by Charlemagne's death. By this point, though, the pope had a larger group of followers and protectors, and when conspirators attacked him again, he did not offer the same mercy. Instead, he sentenced all of those who conspired against him to death.

Necessary Reforms to Unite the People

It was unfortunate that the tentative empire Charlemagne created did not persist beyond his rule because he enacted a number of changes that greatly benefited the people under his control. His reign is often referred to as the Carolingian Renaissance, named after the dynasty which his father began. All of the vital systems of society were reformed to work across all of the lands under his control: the military, government, monetary system, and religion. This gave the people under him a reason to unite because there was now a single person in control and one who implemented changes that made life easier for them.

There was also a literary revival that followed the works of the 4th-century Roman Empire. It is likely that many of the architectural innovations that occurred during the latter half of the Middle Ages were inspired by the art and architecture that began under Charlemagne's rule. He also encouraged reading and scriptural studies. Unfortunately, this cultural revival was limited to the elites who benefited the most by that rebirth.

However, Charlemagne was not averse to learning what other cultures had to offer. As he became exposed to other peoples who lived along his borders, such as the Lombards, Muslims, and Anglo-Saxons, he learned from them. Classic works were both preserved and recopied so that they would not be lost to time. Many of these works are still in existence today, thanks to his forethought to ensure that they didn't disappear.

His economic reform was the most practical change during his reign. He continued reforms that his father had started and finally got rid of the gold sou system. He opted to work with King Offa, the Anglo-Saxon King of Mercia, to establish a system that was based on a metal that was more common than the incredibly rare gold. The new system was the livre carolinienne, which was based on silver.

His other reforms helped to reshape Western Europe, bringing a more unified outlook to all of the major systems. It was like a soft reboot of the Roman Empire, but it would not last. Without Charlemagne, there was no empire. Some of his reforms continued, but some were lost as people again began to try to claim power for themselves instead of working together to continue to grow and prosper.

Chapter 8 – The Treaty of Verdun and the Rurik Dynasty – Beginnings of Modern Nations

Charlemagne's empire started dissolving soon after his death. His son, Louis the Pious, was able to keep the empire going, but the problems that had begun during his father's reign became exacerbated, and he added some new problems of his own creation. When he decided to divide the empire into three different territories for his three remaining sons to rule, it was the beginning of the end of Charlemagne's unified empire.

The Start of Dissolution

Like the Lombards, Louis divided his realm into subkingdoms so that they were easier to govern. During the last few years of Charlemagne's reign, rebellion and corruption had begun to show. Charlemagne even expressed his disillusionment at the way things had soured as he asked his closest companions if the people really were Christian since the corruption and behavior of the people did not suit his ideas of how a Christian people governed by that religion should act.

Charlemagne's son, Louis the Pious, became the ruler after his death in 778 CE. Louis had taken Charlemagne's questioning of the people to heart and focused on reforming the empire to align it more with Christian values, earning him the name Louis the Pious. He developed a blueprint for the way he wanted Christianity to help shape the laws and culture of the people in the empire. Despite efforts by some people within the empire who wanted to remove him, Louis was able to keep his father's empire largely intact.

His largest problem was trying to decide his successor. Louis I had three sons: Pepin, Louis "the German," and Lothair. When he had a fourth son in 823 CE with his second wife, some of his subjects used this to help upset his three sons. His sons, some plotting nobles, and Pope Gregory IV lured Louis to a meeting where they tried to force his abdication. With few options, he agreed and stepped down in 833 CE. This proved to have the opposite effect of what the plotters had expected as it soon became apparent that the rule of his three sons, the pope, and the nobles was not an improvement. By 834, the people had not only decided that his sons had mistreated Louis but that the sons and the people who supported them had no idea how to rule over their territories. The petty infighting was hardly the worst problem, as violence across the realm grew following Louis' abdication, and the population began to demand that Louis be restored.

Louis came back into power in March 834, and he punished those who had instigated his abdication, although his three sons were still his designated heirs. However, Louis did decide to give Aquitaine to his fourth son, Charles, after the death of his eldest son Pepin in 838 CE. Lothair was given Italy, and instead of causing further problems for his father, Lothair put all of his energies into ruling his territory. In 839 CE, Louis accomplished something Charlemagne hadn't—the Byzantine Emperor Theophilus granted him acknowledgment as a great leader of the people. He also commended Louis for his strong defense of Christianity, even though the western and eastern versions of the religion were already growing apart. Despite their differences, both men were still Christians, and they realized that it was more important to focus on that rather than on their differences. Louis the Pious died the next year in June of 840 CE.

Instead of selecting a single person to inherit and rule the empire, Louis opted to divide it. While this was more aligned with Frankish traditions, Charlemagne's decision to keep the empire united proved to be a more stabilizing choice. Louis' decision to divide the nation proved to be far more detrimental to the overall unity of the lands. The sons had already proven that they could not work together to rule when they had forced their father to abdicate. Once Louis was no longer a unifying factor, the squabbles that had marked his sons' previous time as leaders were only amplified.

Open War and an Attempt at Resolving Their Inheritance

Louis I's youngest son, Charles, inherited Aquitaine, something that Louis the German had tried to block when the decision was originally handed down. This had been his brother Pepin's territory prior to his death, and Louis the German had wanted to gain some (if not all) of the territory following Pepin's death. His attempts to change Louis I's mind failed, though, and Charles was made the future leader of Aquitaine. Louis the German was not happy with his lot of ruling over the territory of Bavaria, but there was not much he could do while his father was still alive.

Despite his previous attempts to keep Charles from gaining his own territory, Louis the German chose to side with him after his father's death. The decision was necessary because once their father was gone, Lothair decided that he wanted to reclaim the power that would have been his had he and his brothers not forced Louis' abdication. Unwilling to give up their inheritance, Louis and Charles led a civil war against their brother, which began not long after Louis I died. This bloody civil war lasted until 843 CE. After Louis and Charles first defeated Lothair at Fontenay in 841, they then forced him to flee to Aix-la-Chapelle. Knowing that he could not win, Lothair sought peace.

The Treaty of Verdun was signed in 843 and resulted in Lothair retaining his title of emperor, but he had no control over his brothers' actions as leaders of their own lands. Charles was designated as the ruler over the western region, in an area that today includes France. Lothair kept the middle region of the empire, and he was able to advance the work he had done in Italy while his father was still alive. Louis took the eastern portion of the empire.

Charles appeared to have had the most precarious position because the Vikings were located within his territories, and they were constantly waging battles and razing towns. However, he was able to keep his realm intact and pass it down to his son following his death.

Louis the German chose to divide his lands even more instead of selecting a single successor. The partitioning of a third of the kingdom further degraded the unity that Charlemagne had sought.

Lothair's region appeared to be the least stable because of internal strife. He also divided his realm amongst his sons, and they proved to be just as contentious with each other as Lothair and his brothers had been. Their constant warring against each other led to this portion of the empire coming to ruin.

Ultimately, the division of the empire into thirds played out in a way that helped shape present-day Europe. The region that fell to Charles became the country we now know as France, while Louis' realm became the Holy Roman Empire and eventually Germany. Part of that territory included the region that was under Lothair's control. However, the portion of Lothair's realm eventually evolved into Italy. The Byzantine Empire still controlled the southern part of today's Italy at that time, and they retained that control for a while longer.

The Rurik Dynasty

While the Franks and the Germanic tribes fought over the territories across most of the southern and middle regions of Europe, they largely left the northern area alone. There were some, however, who were not as dissuaded from attempting to occupy this region, despite how cold and desolate it appeared to be. The Varangian chieftain Rurik was one of the few who saw the potential of the largely ignored region in the north.

Not much is known about Rurik because the history was not written down, and over time, it has become impossible to tell what is myth and what is fact. It is possible that he was from one of the Viking settlements and that he chose to go north because it was not nearly as detrimental to his people as it was to the people of the lower half of the continent. This is just speculation, though, as there are no records of his lineage or history.

According to the legends of the founding of modern-day Russia, Rurik led his people north into Ladoga in 862 CE. Rurik and his tribe began to build a settlement that would shelter them through the harsh winters. The settlement of Holmgard was built over the course of the next few years. Based on archeological discoveries, it is likely that this first settlement was south of the city of Novgorod. Although Rurik is the most notable of the dynasty, his two brothers are also remembered as being the founders of the dynasty, often referred to as the Rus' dynasty. According to legend, Rurik died in 879 and was succeeded by Oleg, a relative. Under Oleg, the Rus' territory expanded south. Oleg attacked the Khazars in Kyev and was victorious. Kyev was more developed than the humble beginnings of the Rus' territory, so Oleg decided that it would become a second capital. In the future, the heir apparent of the dynasty would control the original settlement, which would develop into the city of Novgorod, but would reside in Kyev. Over the next century, the dynasty absorbed many of the surrounding tribes. The different cultures and ideologies helped to perpetuate divisions and fractures, but the Rus' dynasty continued to grow over the years, eventually becoming modern-day Russia.

Chapter 9 – Alfred the Great

As with many of the men who rose to power during the early Middle Ages, Alfred the Great, King of Wessex (in what is now Great Britain), did not seem like a likely candidate for the throne. As the fifth son of King Æthelwulf of the West Saxons, he was hardly one of the first choices to become king. His own disinterest seemed like more than enough to keep him from ever ascending to the highest leadership position on the island that would one day become Great Britain.

Perhaps it was this disinterest though that made him such a great leader. Unlike so many of Æthelwulf's other sons who were weak or ineffective rulers—or worse, actively destructive—Alfred accepted the rule that he didn't want and then excelled at doing his job. As one of the first notable rulers on the island, Alfred the Great was able to protect his kingdom from repeated invasions and also reform many established systems to be more efficient. His reign left an indelible mark on the island that would one day form one of the largest empires in the world.

His Early Life and Rise to Power

The early life of Alfred was fairly typical for someone born into the upper class on the island. Born between 847 to 849 CE, he was the fifth son of Æthelwulf of West Saxon. His interest lay in education, particularly literature, but it is likely that his only early education was in the military. As the son of a king, military strategy was certainly something he would be expected to know, even if he was not considered a contender for the throne. By 868, he was in active service in the military and joined King Æthelred I (his brother) in assisting King Burgred of Mercia (another small kingdom on the island). The Danes (more often referred to as Vikings today) had arrived in East Anglia around 865, and by 867, they had taken control of Northumbria. However, the Danish refused to fight, and a peace was negotiated. In 871, the Danes again began to expand their grasp over the island, attacking Wessex. Alfred again joined his brother, and they engaged in several battles against the Danish forces. When Æthelred died that same year, Alfred was the next in line for the throne. However, he did not find success in his first battle against the Danes as the new king. The peace that followed the Battle of Wilton did give the Danish invaders time to pause and consider their options. While they had not failed in the battle, the West Saxon forces proved to offer more resistance than the Danes had likely anticipated. For the next five years, the Danes held off instigating any more battles against the new king.

Resumption of Hostilities

By 876, the Danes were ready to resume their assault on the southwestern region of modern-day England. Their attacks did begin in 876, but they pulled back for a while in 877 because they had accomplished very little with their skirmishes. Perhaps the five years that they had refrained from attacking Alfred and his military made them underestimate their opponent. Or perhaps during that time Alfred had spent more time ensuring that his military was ready for battle. Because the Danes had been so problematic throughout his entire life, there is little doubt that Alfred knew that they would try again to expand into his kingdom.

A third explanation could be that the Danes wanted to gain the element of surprise. The year 878 had barely started when they again attacked Wessex. During that initial push, they were able to take control of Chippenham, resulting in the majority of Alfred's forces relenting. It was said that all of the West Saxons submitted to the Danes with the exception of their king. Over the course of the next few weeks, Alfred reminded the Danes of his presence through guerilla warfare. As he hounded the Danes with his random attacks, Alfred also managed to assemble enough men to have a new army to support him less than two months after Easter. With his men, King Alfred defeated the Danes at the Battle of Edington. Following their surrender, the Danish King Guthrum agreed to be baptized into the Christian religion.

Following this last defeat, Alfred was left free to control the other aspects of his kingdom until 885 when the East Anglian Danes began to attack his kingdom. It took him a year, but in 886, Alfred was able to turn the tide and go on the offensive against this new threat. When he was able to take London, all of the British people who were not residing in Danish-held lands around the city chose to acknowledge Alfred as their rightful king. Alfred may not have continued to press the Danes, but his son, Edward the Elder, was able to use the leverage that Alfred had gained by taking London to push farther into the Danish territories after he became king.

One of the primary reasons that Alfred did not continue to stretch his kingdom across the southern part of the island was because the Danes began to plan new invasions of the island from the continent. This new round of invasions lasted from 892 to 896, and Alfred proved, once again, that his successes in warfare were not a fluke. His ability to take defensive positions made it incredibly difficult for the Danes to gain any new ground. Any time Alfred had any available resources, he had old structures (particularly forts) strengthened, and he had new ones built in more strategic areas. He ensured that their defensive posts were perpetually manned, leaving little chance for the Danes to launch a successful surprise attack. Alfred started having his own ships built in 875, so when new waves of invaders came, he was able to meet them and drive them back.

A secure defense was not his only military strength. Alfred understood that he needed the other peoples on the island, and he maintained a positive relationship with the rulers of Mercia and Wales. When they required assistance, he provided them with support, and they reciprocated in turn.

Beyond the Wars

It is easy to focus on what Alfred achieved as a military man, but his strengths went well beyond just fighting. Since his interest lay more in traditional education and literature, he learned how to govern based on what other great rulers had done. He used the example of rulers like Charlemagne to restructure the different systems in the kingdom, such as the financial and justice systems, making them more efficient.

He was also intent on making sure that those in power did not exploit or oppress the weak or lower-class people of his kingdom. The practice of feuding was restricted (it could not be entirely banned as it was part of the culture, but he did seek to minimize the bloodshed that came out of the practice).

However, it was his reverence for learning that really set Alfred apart from other leaders. He believed that the Viking raids were a sign from the Christian god that people needed to repent for their sins. As long as they sinned, the Vikings would continue to attack. During the period of peace between 878 and 885, he had scholars join him at court so that they could impart more knowledge and instruct him and others in Latin. However, he did encourage all kinds of learning; he knew that if people understood the different systems and points of view others had, people would be far less likely to fight each other. He required all freemen who had time to learn to read English so that they could read books that would give them useful and religious knowledge.

Although he was a very capable military leader, it was the changes that he made within the empire itself while keeping his people safe from repeated attacks that earned Alfred the epithet "the Great." More than just a knowledgeable military strategist, Alfred was a humanitarian and sought to improve the lives of the people across England. He would be remembered for centuries as the ideal king.

Chapter 10 – Otto 1 and the Founding of a Loose Federation

The death of Charlemagne resulted in Western Europe again being plunged into divided regions. However, his reign was not the only time when Western Europe was united. Charlemagne may be the more famous example, but Emperor Otto I gained about the same amount of prestige and unity across Europe. Unlike Charlemagne, Otto I was able to establish an empire that was more permanent—it became known as the Holy Roman Empire. Some historians cite Charlemagne as the source of the empire, but there was a definite break in the territories following his death. What Otto I established lasted for several hundred years, well into the early modern era.

The success of Otto I might be attributed to his more selfish motives in establishing his empire. His beginnings were much humbler than Charlemagne's beginnings, and he had to fight to reach the position of king. Charlemagne was a religious man; Otto I was not particularly religious. There were a number of differences between them, but ultimately, they were both strong leaders who were able to command a military and unite many of the lands that had once been a part of the Western Roman Empire.

From Near Obscurity to Complete Control

Born to one of the Saxon dukes, Otto was one of many people who could possibly become king. It was not a position that he was ever guaranteed to gain, particularly as the Saxons would select a king (it wasn't hereditary) upon the death of the current king. When he was born in 912 CE, he was the second son to a duke. Much of his early years are completely unknown because his position was too minor to track.

During his teenage years, Otto displayed his natural skill in the military. It is speculated that he was initially involved in the campaigns of his father, King Henry the Fowler, against neighboring Germanic tribes. When he was eighteen years old, Otto married Eadgyth, an English lady from a noble family. Together they had a daughter and a son.

Having seen his son's ability to lead, the duke appointed his son to be his successor. While he went by the title of King Henry, Otto's father ruled a small portion of the Saxon territories, not the entire people. When Henry died in 936, the Saxons had to approve of the late king's choice to elevate his second son to the highest position they could offer. They agreed that Otto was a good choice, and he was elected that same year. His coronation occurred in Cologne at Aachen. This location may have been chosen because it was said to have been Charlemagne's residence, even after he was crowned emperor in Italy.

Otto immediately was pressed to exhibit his military prowess as his neighbors tested his abilities to see if they could take over his territory. The feuding and fighting would have been detrimental to a less capable leader, but Otto had been prepared to fight wars in his early years, and it was this early demonstration of his abilities that assured his people that he was the right choice. The biggest test to his power actually came from within his own family. His elder brother and other members of the family were not satisfied because they had been overlooked for the position of king, and they plotted against Otto for years to come.

Otto was just as effective against his family as he was against outsiders who questioned his authority. His father had been passable as a leader, but he never fully controlled his people or the other dukes within his domain. Otto did not have the same problem. As soon as he ascended to the role of king, he began to consolidate power, removing the power that the dukes had enjoyed which had so irked his father. This move ultimately benefited Otto, but in the beginning, the dukes fought against the loss of the power they had enjoyed for so long.

A year after his coronation (937 CE), Otto's half-brother, Thankmar, formed an alliance with some of the other dukes who were dissatisfied with what Otto was doing. Their attempt to remove him ended in an abysmal loss. Thankmar was killed during the battle. One of the dukes who had sided with him was deposed, and the second, Duke Eberhard of Franconia, claimed to submit to Otto's authority. He soon proved that he had been lying when Otto's younger brother Henry followed the same path as Thankmar.

The next revolt occurred two years later in 939 CE. Unlike Thankmar, Henry sought additional help from outside sources, and he gained the backing of the king of France, Louis IV. The two dukes who sided with Henry, Duke Eberhard and Duke Gilbert of Lotharingia, died. Otto was then faced with passing judgment on his younger brother. In what may have looked like a weakness, he opted to forgive Henry instead of having him executed. Henry was allowed to stay by Otto's side.

In repayment for this, Henry led a new rebellion against his brother because he was convinced that he would make a better ruler than Otto. Instead of attempting another battle, he coordinated with other conspirators to assassinate Otto. Unfortunately for Henry, Otto learned what he was planning, and in 941, all of those who conspired with Henry were executed. Twice Henry had tried to remove Otto from power, and twice everyone who plotted with him was killed. However, Otto, yet again, forgave his brother.

And this time he was right to do so.

In the years following this second attempt on Otto's crown, Henry became one of his staunchest supporters. His loyalty to his older brother did not waver again. It probably helped that Otto gave Henry more land; even while his brother and the dukes were conspiring against him, Otto continued to expand his reach. These new territories were divided between other members of Otto's family, showing just how much he favored and valued them.

The first group he was able to defeat were the Slavs who resided just east of Otto's kingdom. During 950, Otto defeated one of his primary rivals, Prince Boleslav I of Bohemia. The prince's life was spared, but he had to agree to pay tribute to Otto going forward. Next, Otto turned his attention to the problematic region that would one day be France. The people to the west were constantly attacking Otto's borders because they believed that Lotharingia (Lorraine) was theirs. Their claims meant nothing, though, as they were not able to take the territory from Otto.

In 951, Otto began considering a campaign to conquer the place where the Roman Empire had begun. He marched his men into northern Italy in a bid to take the lands that had once been a part of the Lombard Kingdom. He was given justification when Adelaide (the widow of the nominal king of Italy) requested his assistance. King Lothair II had died, and the people of Italy did not support her to fill his role. King Berengar II (the current king of Italy and possible murderer of King Lothair) had taken her prisoner and was holding her to try to gain control over her husband's lands. Otto marched to her aid, likely with the intention of marrying her. His wife had died six years earlier, making an alliance through marriage possible. If Adelaide agreed to the marriage, she would again have the stability that was lost by her husband's death, and Otto would expand his domain even farther without having to resort to an all-out war, which would have bred resentment among the Italian people. Otto now had a chance to be a hero who would be welcomed for having saved Adelaide and given her people a strong leader. He successfully rescued and married the widow. The title of King of Italy was then appended to the many titles he had earned since he had risen to power.

There was one more internal problem that he had to face, and that was his son. Now an adult, Liudolf sought to gain power in his own name. By working with other Germanic figures, Liudolf rebelled against his father back home. For the first time in his life, Otto was now facing a family member who posed a real threat to his throne. Both his half-brother and his brother had been inferior fighters, but Liudolf had learned from Otto himself, making him a much more formidable opponent. However, Otto was well aware of a problem that his son neglected to consider during his revolt. While Otto could not successfully face his son back home, he could simply wait for the Magyars to attack his realm, a people that some historians believe were descended from the infamous Attila hordes. They were restless, and Otto knew that they would pose a problem to Saxony; all he had to do was let his son deal with the threat. In 954, the Magyars invaded the region where Liudolf and his supporters were staying. Unable to face both the Magyars and his father, Liudolf was forced to submit to his father in 955. Again in full control of his home, Otto quickly defended his lands from the Magyars during the Battle of Lechfeld. The defeat was so destructive to the Magyars that they avoided the Germanic regions in the future.

Turning His Attention to the Future

Otto's natural leadership and military abilities had given him an advantage that no one had enjoyed since Charlemagne. Unlike the legendary man, Otto faced both external and internal strife during his entire life, and he always succeeded. Despite not being a religious man, Otto did show a kind of mercy (although he seemed to extend it primarily to members of his family) that was not obvious under Charlemagne. This was perhaps why he was able to forge a unity that was able to continue even after his demise.

Having seen other empires and kingdoms crumble (and having been the person to bring about the end to some of them), Otto knew that he needed to establish a succession that would be able to keep his work intact after his death. In 961, he chose the son that he had with Adelaide to be his successor. This son was also named Otto, and when his father decided that he would be the next to rule over the realm, he was only six years old. To ensure that no one would question his decision, Otto held elections to legitimize his choice. When his chosen son was elected to be his successor, the elder Otto had him crowned to be a joint ruler.

Satisfied that his legacy would be continued and that his son would learn to rule by working side-by-side with him, Otto returned to Italy to face the latest round of problems that King Berengar II had stirred up against the pope. When he successfully mitigated the problems in 962, Pope John XII followed the precedent set by Pope Leo III and crowned Otto Emperor of the Holy Roman Empire. To combat any criticism, the pope issued the Privilegium Ottonianum, which dictated the relationship that would exist between the new emperor and the pope. A year later, Pope John XII worked with King Berengar II to try to remove Otto from the office that the pope had just bestowed on him. Incensed by this, Otto first defeated Berengar in yet another battle. Once that problem was solved, Otto I turned his attention to the pope. Since he was not a religious man, Otto did not have the same respect or reverence for the position that Charlemagne had held for it. Otto had the pope removed from his position and selected the pope himself. His choice became Pope Leo VIII. He did not remain the pope for long though, dying in 965. Otto again chose a new pope, this time John XIII, a figure who was already widely disliked among the leaders of the Church. The revolt against Otto's choice was almost immediate, and he was again forced to return to Italy to put down another revolt.

Since Italy had repeatedly proven to be a troublesome place, Otto I decided to remain there for several years to ensure that no new problems would arise. His absence had made people more prone to turn to rebellion, so he was removing that temptation by being physically present and ruling his other lands from Italy. Seeing an opportunity to possibly extend his domain even farther, he traveled into places that were under the Byzantine Empire's dominion, although he had no success in expanding into the east.

Realizing that he needed to focus on the future of the lands that he already had, Otto I worked to secure his son's leadership. A marriage with Theophanu (either the niece or the daughter of the emperor of the Byzantine Empire) was arranged in 972. Instead of defeating the Byzantine Empire through fighting, Otto was going to have his son marry into their family, solidifying a more stable alliance that he hoped would help his son in retaining his position. The next year, 973 CE, Otto I died.

An Unexpected Legacy

Otto I's abilities as a leader and military strategist are undeniable, but they were not his only strengths. Under his rule, the lands experienced a second renaissance. His lack of spirituality did not mean that he did not understand the value of those people who dedicated their lives to the Church. By appointing people who really cared for their communities to positions of power, he provided the people all across his empire with the support that they had not had since Charlemagne. Their cultures began to thrive, and architecture began to evolve into what became the signature look of the Middle Ages. The progress during the second half of the Middle Ages can largely be attributed to the work that was done under Otto I. By removing the constant petty squabbles, skirmishes, and battles that plagued various regions, the peoples under his rule could now find enough stability to focus on education, culture, and literature.

Otto I's realm was not as large as the one that Charlemagne acquired, but it lasted far longer after his death. Some historians credit Charlemagne as the first Holy Roman Emperor, but that is a difficult argument to make since the unity under his rule did not last beyond his death. Otto I ensured that his legacy would not be snuffed out when he died, and his son went on to rule over the lands that Otto I had conquered. The Holy Roman Empire would certainly change and shift over time, and it would never be a cohesive nation, like France, Spain, or England. It was more of a loose federation with different leaders vying for power, but they did retain a similar culture and identity well into the early modern era. What emerged over the years was far more similar to what Otto I had established than the more solid unity that Charlemagne had sought.

Chapter 11 – The Reign of Venice

Venice rose to prominence during the first half of the Middle Ages and remained an important city well into the early modern era. During most of the reign of the Roman Empire and immediately after the fall of Rome, the region of modern-day Venice was largely a community of fishermen and salt workers. Following the invasion of the Lombards in northern Italy, there was a migration of Italians south, and many of them settled in this region.

For several centuries, the region passed back and forth between being controlled by the Byzantine Empire and whatever group was in control of the lands that are now Italy. By the time of the Crusades, they had become a formidable power all their own. Sometimes the people, more specifically those in power in Venice, caused problems for the pope and the cardinals in Rome.

The Veneti

Before the fall of Rome, a Celtic people lived along the coast of northeastern Italy, and they enjoyed the protection of Rome as its citizens. However, the invasion of the Huns caused the people to panic. Hoping to escape the horrors left in the wake of the Huns, the Celtic people fled to the lagoon and settled on the islands. Without Rome, they were forced to develop their own federation that ensured they would protect each other. Since they had settled on the islands, the people were more isolated and less tempting to the constant flow of people trying to pick up the scraps of territories after the fall of Rome.

With the arrival of the Lombards in Italy, the islands found that their population began to significantly increase. The Italians on the mainland were trying to escape the marching Lombards who easily took over much of northern Italy. For the next couple hundred years, the people were under the control of the Byzantine Empire.

Seeking Independence and Establishing a New Government

By 726 CE, Venice began to move away from the empire and establish a modicum of independence. To establish their own government, they elected a doge (duke) named Orso Ipato. He made an anti-Byzantine declaration, earning him the respect and awe of the people. While he was able to rule, there was no line of succession established or any method of electing new officials. As a result, the Byzantine Empire set up their own officials again once he was gone.

This state of affairs lasted until the beginning of the 750s when the Exarchate of Ravenna ended. The Byzantine Empire stopped fighting against the Lombards, losing some of their territories. Most of the rest of the century was spent in political chaos as the people in powerful positions in Venice switched between wanting to be a part of the empire and wanting to be independent. Other powers from the surrounding regions also began to eye Venice as being in a potentially useful position, most notably the Church.

In a bid to end the perpetual swings in power, Doge Obelerio allied with the Franks. Working with his brother, Doge Obelerio worked to set up some measure of control for themselves, which they thought would be easier to accomplish under the Franks. They allied themselves with King Pepin (the first son of Louis I) and wanted to finally rid Venice of Byzantine influence.

This obviously upset the powerful families that did not want to see the duchy removed from the empire. To solve this problem, the Parteciaco family lost their governmental seat, and it was transferred to the Rialto Islands.

When the Franks and the Byzantine Empire finally agreed on the Franco-Byzantine treaty in 814, most of Venice's problems were resolved. The treaty assured the duchy that they would have their own political and juridical independence. This guarantee was more than they had previously gotten from the empire, but it did not remove them from their control. Roughly 25 years later, the doge had accumulated enough power to be able to make agreements with outside powers without requiring consent or permission from the Byzantine Empire.

At this point, the small Duchy of Venice was in a unique position. They straddled the two worlds of the Byzantine Empire and the ever-changing powers in Western Europe. This made them a prime location for merchants and traders to live and conduct their trade. Residing in an area that was easy to access from the Mediterranean, Venice was a logical place for shipping. As they had enough autonomy to make decisions, they could be used to go around restrictions placed on the various continental powers. Over time, Venice became a highly influential power, and some of its people became very wealthy.

The people of Venice realized that the doge required some oversight and governmental balance to keep the duchy from becoming his own little kingdom. A ruling class naturally developed from the constant flow of trade and wealth that spread throughout the duchy, giving a check to the power of the doge. Over time, the population began to develop their own cultures and a sense of regional consciousness that was more aligned with a nation than a duchy. The 9th century saw the duchy become more democratic as the doge was again elected into the position instead of it being a hereditary position.

This singular history helped to create a people who were less beholden to the pope and more able to negotiate in their own interests. The duchy had learned how to be clever and manipulative of outside powers, and Venice eventually became a rival of Rome in terms of the power that it had. At times, the Duchy of Venice even manipulated the decrees of various popes for its own gain. Perhaps the most serious of these was when the people of Venice essentially took control over one of the later Crusades. Instead of heading into the Muslim lands like they had originally planned to do, the Venetians took the Crusaders to Constantinople and sacked the city. That was the beginning of the end of the Byzantine Empire, and it was made possible because of how powerful the Duchy of Venice had become. It was this unique position of not really belonging anywhere that gave this small settlement a chance at becoming a city that was one of the most influential in Western Europe for several decades.

Chapter 12 – The Vikings

Among all of the most famous (or perhaps infamous) peoples of the early Middle Ages, the Vikings stand out as one of the most barbaric and mysterious. People tend to think they know enough about the Vikings, but as soon as you start to look into their history, lore, and systems, it is nearly impossible not to get lost as you dig deeper and deeper to learn more. They were a group that was much more complex and diverse than most people realize.

In addition to being a dangerous enemy, the Vikings were curious explorers who managed to do something that no one else in Europe achieved until the early modern age: The Vikings actually reached what would one day be known as North America. Not only did they reach North America, but they also made no attempt to conquer or explore it. Their behavior toward the native peoples was significantly different from those of the future explorers from other parts of Europe.

The Beginning of a Mythical Time – The Viking Age

The legendary Danish fighters that we now call the Vikings were unique in many ways compared to the groups of people around them. The leaders of the neighboring lands and kingdoms attacked each other largely over territory, trying to obtain more power by taking parts of continental Europe from each other. The Vikings were notoriously a seafaring people whose ferocity and curiosity took them far from home and well away from their homes in Denmark, Norway, and Sweden where they originally lived.

One of the reasons that they are so well known (or at least why their name is still known to nearly everyone in Western civilization) is because they were ferocious warriors. For more than three centuries (the 8th to the 11th), the Vikings attacked their neighbors and sailed across the channel to what is now England to constantly raid and plunder and take those stolen goods back to their homes. They journeyed far from home both to the east and west, and they left remnants of their settlements in Russia and in northern parts of Canada.

When the Vikings were attacking, the people knew it. The Vikings were much like fictitious dragons that adorned the bows of their ships—you could see them a long way off, and there was often very little that anyone could do to stop them. They were a force that proved difficult to quell, and more often than not, they were victorious in their raids.

The period between the 8th and 11th centuries is called the Viking Age by many historians because of their dominance. Their first known raid occurred in 793 on the island of Lindisfarne, off the northeastern coast of England. This was the location of a monastery, and the Vikings were as merciless toward this wealthy monastery as they were anywhere else that they attacked. It showed that they were among the few tribes that did not care about the sanctity of the Christian religion, and they were just as willing to plunder the religious buildings as they did the towns and villages they attacked. The Christians tended to hoard most of their wealth in their religious establishments and relied on the fact that they were religious places to protect them, making them easy and profitable targets. To be fair, though, even the Germanic Visigoths who had sacked Rome had left the cathedrals alone. However, the one failing with this way of thinking was that the Visigoths had been Christians—the Vikings were not. There was no reason for the monks who lived on Lindisfarne to think that the fiercely decorated ships were any real threat until the Vikings had actually landed.

Their Origins and Known History

What drove the people who were once ordinary farmers and tradesmen into becoming such fierce and prolific fighters is unknown. Since the Vikings did not keep written records, what is known about them is largely through the lens of the people they raided. In the early days, the Vikings attacked the people who lived in coastal towns and monasteries. Like the dragons depicted on their ships, the Vikings arrived, attacked, and then left in a space of time that was unheard of until then. There were no other types of raiders like them in Europe. Battles and warfare around Europe included having time for the target town or city to set up defenses and counter the attacks, but the Vikings were far too efficient and tactical in their targets. They operated more like an incredibly well-organized group of bandits, yet they were definitely a type of military force. Their method of attacking was more like a bolt of lightning than a long, protracted storm. With many of the wars on continental Europe not amounting to much more than what the armies could take from the places they invaded, the end results between the Viking raids and the perpetual wars really weren't that different. The difference was that the Vikings weren't seeking to rule over the places they raided.

Without a written account of what drove them to attack the Lindisfarne monastery, historians are left to speculate about the reasons that drove them to attack coastal areas. Among the most likely theories are a lack of food and resources or perhaps even the lack of enough farmlands, driving some of the people to seek a way to supplement their assets. It is also possible that there may have been too many males, and the best way to occupy younger sons was to send them to acquire valuable items that would benefit the whole community. They certainly would have faced oppression and persecution for being pagans instead of Christians. This would not only explain why they targeted so many monasteries and churches, but it would also cause the Christians to question why their god was constantly failing them against such an inferior foe. Given how far away from home the Vikings traveled, it is also incredibly likely that they were both curious and adventurous long before it was in vogue in the rest of Europe.

Even stranger, the Vikings were not always out raiding and plundering. Many of them continued to work their fields or ply their trades much of the year. During harvest times, coastal Europe rested easier because most of the Vikings were too preoccupied with agricultural pursuits to attack. Over time, some Vikings began to choose to raid with the majority of their time, becoming something like full-time soldiers or mercenaries (except that they were paid in what they could take instead of through military funding).

Nor were they afraid of the cold that most Europeans seemed to avoid. By settling in places like Iceland and trying to establish themselves in Greenland, the Vikings chose to live in places that others were not likely to go. They were also amazing merchants who knew how to trade for better bargains with their goods. Since they lived in areas that were exotic, they had an abundance of items that were scarce elsewhere. They also traded in slaves, which was still incredibly common in Europe at that time.

Changing the History of the Continent

While they were definitely a force to be reckoned with, the Vikings eventually did settle down, spreading across the northern part of Europe, including England, Scotland, Ireland, Russia, and Iceland. Their main purpose (at least in the early days) usually wasn't to take control of the places they attacked. However, this changed over time, with modern-day England being the most obvious example of the Vikings settling down in a place that was already occupied.

Charlemagne and some rulers who would follow him over the next few centuries tried to force Christian conversion on all pagans, but that really did not work with the Vikings. The Danes firmly held onto their own intricate religion that today is known as Norse mythology. While Norse mythology is a bit depressing, their beliefs were every bit as storied, entertaining, and complex as the Greek and Roman mythologies. After seeing the inequality that the Christians perpetuated in their trading and contracts despite their religion, the Vikings very likely felt that their raids were justified. They were not going to listen to people who believed in a religion that taught peace and tolerance but practiced the exact opposite. Those who continued to trade with Christians often adorned themselves with Christian accessories (such as a cross necklace or clothing) during deals so that they would be treated as a Christian. Upon arriving home, the Vikings would remove the Christian accessories and put on gear with Norse mythological symbols. For a long time, the Vikings knew enough about Christianity to practice it alongside their own religion so that they were not persecuted.

Over time, the Vikings began to settle in some of the places that they had frequently raided. Migrating into Russia, they were among the first to settle the cold lands. However, it is England where their presence was the most influential. The Vikings were a perpetual problem for Alfred the Great, but they also knew the value of peace.

There was a period of peace between the Danes who occupied the island and the native people, and they came to see that Alfred actually practiced many of the things that the Christian religion taught. Alfred worked for the betterment of his people, unlike so many Christian leaders who were largely focused on their own power and wealth. Eventually, the Vikings made peace with Alfred, though the king did have to make peace with different groups of Vikings since they were not a single society. Alfred also saw that the Vikings were much more than just raiding parties. The Danes had established trade centers across the island, and they were expert traders, attracting the business of many other powers. Over time, Alfred's military strength and wisdom as a ruler convinced the Danes to stop fighting. Eventually, they became a part of English society. This close proximity and positive relationship helped many Vikings to willingly convert to Christianity over the centuries.

There was a similar shift across the continent. The trade centers that the Vikings established all along the coast eventually led them to get to know the Christians around them and peacefully convert. Although it was a gradual process, it was a choice that the Vikings made themselves. They could not be forced to convert, but they could be convinced through the same displays of loyalty and tolerance that was a part of the early days of Christianity. This is fortunate because the melding of the Vikings with their neighbors meant that their histories and mythology were finally recorded. Today we know far more about this legendary people because of the relationships they developed with other Europeans.

A Jaunt Across an Ocean

Similar to Christopher Columbus, the Vikings' landing in North America was not intentional. The first time the Vikings were made aware of the existence of a new land was when Bjarni Herjólfsson was trying to reach Greenland. His ship was blown far off course, and when he and his men saw land to the west, they took note before turning around and finally reaching Greenland. Upon reaching their destination, he talked about what he had seen to the son of Erik the Red. This man was Leif Erikson. Erikson was curious to learn more about this unknown land, and in 1000 CE, he took a crew of men to travel about 1,800 miles to explore it by traversing the same path that Bjarni had taken.

Upon their arrival, Erikson and his men called the place Vinland, after their home Greenland. The natives were far more hostile than they had perhaps anticipated, and the settlement failed. Considering the distance from their home, it is probable that Erikson decided that it was not worth trying to keep the settlement going, as it was far too costly and impractical to try to settle on such a wild and distant land. His curiosity perhaps sated, the men returned home with the knowledge of a place that the rest of Europe didn't discover for another 500 years.

The Vikings had a reputation for being incredibly vicious, yet they weren't nearly as vicious toward the native peoples as the Europeans were once they realized that they could exploit the Americas. The Vikings were clever and knew their limitations. They did not seek to rule new lands or force their ideas on others. They were surviving through whatever means were necessary or required. When their needs were met, they wandered and learned about the world around them. They did not flaunt their ideas, learnings, or discoveries, choosing to simply keep the information to themselves. They were a people who were far more complex and varied than fiction and modern sources tend to portray them.

Chapter 13 – The Second Half of the Middle Ages

The second half of the Middle Ages saw a lot of changes across the continent, some of them incredibly positive. However, it is the horrors and tragedies that people tend to remember. These were the events that were passed down in tales and are often repeated in fiction today.

The Great Schism – Christianity Officially Divided

Christianity had pretty much spread all across the Roman Empire by the time Rome was sacked by the Visigoths. The more popular the religion became, the more diverse the beliefs were about Jesus and what he preached. There were several attempts to make a more unified form of Christianity, but despite those attempts, different sects still developed across Europe. While most of these sects were largely stamped out, the differences between Eastern and Western Christianity continued to grow. Eventually, the beliefs were so diverse that the powers in Rome and Constantinople could no longer overlook those differences.

The division between the two versions of Christianity was inevitable. Constantinople continued with many of the same powers and ideas that had been the hallmark of Rome. As they had been a part of the Roman Empire, people in the Byzantine Empire considered themselves a continuation of that empire. It is only during the modern era that they started being called the Byzantine Empire. In comparison, Western Europe became divided, with rulers acting like vultures picking over the corpse of Rome. Because they had not only managed to remain intact and thriving but also expanded the empire into new territories, the spiritual leaders in the Byzantine Empire believed that their way was the right way. However, they were very tolerant of people in their empire who practiced Western Christianity and believed its precepts.

For the people of Western Europe, a common form of Christianity was all they had to keep them united. While there were other sects, such as the Arian Christians, most were Nicaean. They had only one leader, the pope, and they believed that he was the direct spiritual successor to St. Paul. They were less tolerant of the eastern form of Christianity, just as they were intolerant of Arians and other sects. They did manage to live in peace for a few centuries.

That all changed in the middle of the 11th century.

In 1053 CE, Pope Leo IX angered Patriarch Michael I Cerularius (the head of the Eastern Church) when he tried to claim leadership over all of the Christian world, including the Christians of the Byzantine Empire. To prove that he was in control, Leo IX gave the Eastern Churches in southern Italy the choice to either conform to Western Christianity or be shut down. There was absolutely no chance Patriarch Michael would agree to this (and certainly no reason as he was much more powerful). Michael was incensed by the pope's actions, and in retaliation for the pope's power grab, Michael had all the churches that preached Western Christianity shut down in Constantinople.

Leo thought that he could strongarm Michael into bending to the will of the Western Church and sent representatives to Constantinople to try to exercise his authority. The fact that he had to send emissaries to try to accomplish his dictate should have told him who had more power, but Leo was blinded by his own belief in his religion to see the world for the way it really was. His representatives arrived in Constantinople in 1054. His primary representative, Cardinal Humbert, marched into the Hagia Sophia, a more opulent and impressive structure than anything that could be found in Rome, and placed a papal bull on the altar during one of the patriarch's services. The bull stated that the patriarch and all of his followers had been excommunicated by the pope. It is possible that the bull was not issued by the pope though, as he had died not long after his representatives left Rome. Cardinal Humbert was an incredibly aggressive member of the Western Church, and he hated the people of the Byzantine Empire. They lived much easier and opulent lives, and it is probable that he was incredibly jealous. Being in their capital provided him with a chance to really insult them, and the papal bull may have been his attempt to do just that. Again, Michael retaliated with the same measure, excommunicating all those who practiced Western Christianity.

The widening gap between the two sides of the same religion became a chasm that has never been mended. Referred to as the Great Schism, the events started by Pope Leo IX irrevocably divided Christianity into two different religions, the Roman Catholic and the Greek Orthodox Churches. Despite several attempts during the next century and a half after these events to bring the two Christian religions back into a single one, the animosity between the two made it impossible for the powerful men of each religion to ever forgive the other side. During the rest of the Middle Ages, their differences ensured that they did not reconcile, despite that being one of the founding principles preached by Jesus.

Crusading for Christ – Nearly 200 Years of Fighting

There is perhaps no better illustration of just how much animosity was built up over the centuries between the two Christian religions than the Crusades. Less than 50 years after the events that initiated the Great Schism, the first Crusade began. The two religions may have disliked each other, but they both hated the Muslims more. Removing the Muslims from the Holy Land was something that both the Roman Catholic and Greek Orthodox Churches could agree to do together. For the Catholics, it was a chance to repent for their sins and gain recognition, and for the Catholic pope, it was a way to consolidate his power in Western Europe. For the Byzantine Empire, it was a way to take back lands that had been taken from them during the Muslim expansion across the Near East and Northern Africa. Their motivations may not have been altruistic (and were certainly quite selfish for the pope and patriarch), but it was one of the few times that the two religions agreed to work together. They had some marginal and temporary successes, and it was the only Crusade that could be said to be successful on any level.

Historians disagree on how many Crusades there were because they became a very regular occurrence. Between 1095 (the first Crusade), nearly 200 years would pass before the final Crusade. As the reasons for the Crusades became less clear and the Crusaders less organized, there were more opportunities for corruption.

The best instance of this corruption was the Crusade that was carried out between 1202 and 1204. The Crusaders were supposed to go and try to reclaim the Holy Land, but it was quickly repurposed by the Venetians. The Crusaders arrived in and around Venice hoping to make their way to Egypt, but the price that the Venetians demanded to take them across the Mediterranean was too high. Seeing a chance to profit from the Crusade, the Venetians agreed to take them where they wanted to go if the Crusaders would reclaim Zara, Egypt, which was not part of what the pope had told the Crusaders to do. The pope became infuriated at both the actions of the Venetians and the Crusaders, and he excommunicated them all (although he did later rescind the excommunication of the non-Venetians).

It is uncertain what happened to precipitate the next chain of events, but the Venetians ended up going to Constantinople. At first, the Crusaders were in awe of the city that was so much more impressive than anything that they had seen in Western Europe. It was so impressive that they ended up sacking the Byzantine capital, largely out of greed and a vindictive desire to harm the opposing Christian Church. Instead of attacking Muslims, they were now literally attacking fellow Christians. What was lost during this Catholic attack on the Greek Orthodox Church is still mourned today because they took things that had been saved from the fall of Rome. Records and histories were lost because of the avarice of the Crusaders and Venetians. The Byzantine Empire was already in decline, but they never really recovered from this attack. Ironically, the Christians had weakened a part of their own lands, making it much easier for the Muslims to overtake and finally dissolve an entire Christian empire. Essentially, the Christians helped the Muslims instead of attacking them, though it would be the middle of the 15th century before the Byzantine Empire finally ended.

The Crusades had completely lost their original purpose, but they still continued until the end of the 13th century. After this, the Catholic Church did not sanction any more Crusades. Anyone who went to seek glory by attacking the Muslims and trying to reclaim the Holy Land did it without the backing of the Church. More importantly, many of the nations in Europe actually made themselves more vulnerable to attacks by sending their knights and leaders away to fight in lands that were far away. For example, the Holy Roman Empire took England's King Richard the Lionheart prisoner when he was returning from the Crusades. He was only returned after his mother, Eleanor of Aquitaine, paid a hefty ransom. Leaders had to increase taxes on their people to fund the wars, which was far more of a problem to the people than the Muslims occupying the Holy Land was. By the beginning of the 14th century, leaders decided to keep their wars closer to home where they could have some tangible benefits from their wars.

The Wars That Scarred Europe

Warring between the nations was not entirely absent during the Crusades, but they did happen less frequently as many of the best fighters were away participating in the Crusades. England saw an increase in internal strife during this time, including a period called the Anarchy. Like many civil wars, this war was over the succession to the throne. The rightful heir at the beginning of the Anarchy was Henry I's daughter, Adelaide. After her brother's death, she returned to the kingdom; her husband, the Holy Roman Emperor Henry V, had died, and with no other apparent heir, Henry I wanted to make sure she would take his place. Following his death, the nobility who had sworn allegiance to her broke their promise and crowned Stephen of Blois, Henry I's nephew, king. Stephen claimed that the king had changed his mind about the succession on his deathbed, giving Stephen the throne. Between 1135 when Henry I died and 1153 when the head of the Church stepped in, England was embroiled in war as Adelaide, better known as Empress Maude, fought Stephen to take her rightful place. She never got her birthright, but her son, Henry, was made Stephen's successor.

A more devastating war spanned more than 100 years and included most of the European nations. Known as the 100 Years' War, it seemed that the energy that had been put into the Crusades was now being used to kill their fellow Christians instead. Questions of succession were again at the heart of the problem when Charles IV of France died without an heir or a named successor. Historians would call the intermittent fighting between 1337 and 1453 the Hundred Years' War because of how long and ever-changing the war was. Marriages between the royal families of England and France had given English monarchs a claim to the French throne.

England's Edward III had a claim to the throne as the nephew of the late King Charles IV. In a bid to ensure that the English king was not placed on the French throne, the French resorted to citing a couple of old laws that said that succession could not pass through a woman. Since Edward III had been related to Charles through his mother, the laws said that he was excluded from the succession.

Initially, Edward III seemed indifferent to his claim to France because he had enough trouble fighting the Scots. When the chosen ruler, King Philip VI, decided to help agitate the problem by supporting the Scottish King David II, Edward became incensed. This was compounded when King Philip VI took Aquitaine, which was part of England at the time. Edward III was both a clever strategist and an unmerciful enemy. Not only did he decide to reclaim his lands, but he also decided to put forth his claim as the rightful heir to the French throne. He didn't rely just on military might though. Many of the nobles in France did not care for King Philip, and Edward leveraged that to sow discord in France.

England and France would battle for over 120 years, pulling other nations into the fray from time to time. After 80 years (long after Edward and his sons had died), it seemed that England was going to win. This period is when one of the most well-known figures from the era arose: Joan of Arc. She told the French King Charles VII that she had visions that could help him win the war. Charles decided to listen to her, and in doing so, the French were able to finally turn the tides of the war. Though Joan's achievements were few (but still quite impressive considering the fact that she had not been trained and she fought at the front of the battles that she participated in), the victories were what the French needed to feel like they still stood a chance of winning. When the English burned her at the stake in 1431, the French had an even more personal reason to fight. It took almost another 20 years for the war to end, and it never did end up matching the same intensity from previous years. By 1455, England had become embroiled in the War of the Roses, and the 100 Years' War finally came to an end as a different one started.

The constant wars saw many changes in warfare. By the end of the 100 Years' War, knights, who had been essential during the Crusades, were now obsolete. Guns were introduced, entirely changing the tactics of war. The changes in weaponry required a significant change in strategies and military structures since the formations and tactics used by the Romans no longer worked against the evolving weaponry. Military structures came to rely on personnel who were trained and ready to fight (a standing army) instead of relying on peasants and people who knew little about how to fight.

The Dangers of Nature

There were several natural events that almost entirely reshaped Europe during the second half of the Middle Ages. The Great Famine between 1315 and 1317 is still remembered across Europe for its devastating and long-lasting effects on the population. Part of the problem was that the agrarian industry was based on meeting just the current need. Extra food and farming were not considered at a time when the population of the continent was bursting. Life had gotten far simpler, and people began to shift from the familiar agrarian work to trades because there were more than enough people to work the fields. Without having to worry about enough food to survive, artesian trades began to grow, and people began to collect in larger groups that grew into towns. The food supply had been built based on what was optimal instead of a worst-case scenario. In 1315, the spring was particularly wet, making it nearly impossible to plant the next crop based on the usual schedule. The farmers had to wait until the rains stopped, and those who didn't wait lost much of their work because the seeds rotted in the soil which was too wet for them to sprout and grow. With a shorter, later planting season, the crop yield was considerably smaller than previous ones, and it was impossible to meet the need for food. During that year, there were not that many deaths over the winter, but many people did not have adequate food. Malnourished by the next spring, they were unable to keep the schedule needed to meet the demand for food. With fewer people and manpower to tend the fields, there was another shortage during the harvest, and many people died in 1316. Stories such as Hansel and Gretel resulted from this time as families left children in the woods because they could not feed their entire family. The older members of some families opted to starve so that the younger, stronger members of the family had enough food to be able to work the next spring. The famine was so bad by 1317 that even the monarchs in continental Europe felt its effects. Though the spring of 1317 finally returned to the weather they needed, there were far too few people to tend the fields. To make their problems worse, people had resorted to eating seeds to keep from starving, which meant that there were not enough seeds to plant enough crops for the next year. Ailments like tuberculosis and pneumonia claimed many lives as people were too weak to fight off illness. During this time, it is estimated that 10 to 25 percent of the urban population perished.

However, this was not the greatest natural disaster to strike Europe during the Middle Ages.

One of the most notorious pandemics in human history started in far-off China. It spread across Asia and the Middle East, and it reached the Muslim world by the 14th century. By this time, Europe had heard of this deadly illness, but they believed that their Christian god would protect them. As far as they could tell, it was a plague that was affecting pagans, heathens, and anyone who didn't follow the Christian god. They would soon see that they were not immune from what would later be dubbed the Black Death.

The plague most likely arrived in Europe through multiple locations. It is known that the Italian ports were the first to experience the Black Death, which was inevitable since people from around the known world visited them. There were numerous things that contributed to its spread. With the rise of towns, people were living in much smaller spaces that were much closer together. Many of the areas were overcrowded, and the lack of proper hygiene increased the spread of pests like rats and mice, which allowed the plague to spread quickly once it reached a town or city.

Most people are well aware that the Black Death was spread through flea bites, but that wasn't the only way it could spread. Often called the bubonic plague, there were actually three types (or more accurately methods) of plague. Flea bites were the method of transmitting the bubonic strand, which then attacked the lymph nodes. Based on the speed with which the disease spread though, it is certain that people also contracted the pneumonic strand, which was spread through coughing, sneezing, and breathing out the bacteria. There did seem to be some level of dim understanding that the air was unclean around those who contracted the illness. The pope kept the air around him covered in smoke and scents as he had candles and incense burning during the entire scare. The third strand of the plague is the septicemic plague, or blood plague. It is unlikely that this was a common way of transmitting the illness, although some probably did contract this strand as their loved ones bled in the late stages. This contact with their contaminated blood became a death sentence if a person had an open wound. Fleas definitely helped to contribute to the spread of the disease, but once it had reached a town or city, it is just as likely that a person contracted it through the bacteria in the air as through the fleas.

The Black Death returned in waves across Europe over the next few decades, but it was never as devasting as that first time. In the wake of the first wave of the plague, cities learned to implement quarantines, thanks to the ingenuity of the people in Venice. Their success in containing and then avoiding later waves of the Black Death was duplicated all across Europe, and this type of containment is still used today.

Following that first arrival of the plague, historians estimate that between a quarter and a half of the European population perished due to the plague during this time, making it one of the worst disasters in European history. It caused such a deep scar on the European psyche that most people are well aware of the event, even if they don't know much about it.

Chapter 14 – The Renaissance

The Renaissance was a time when the European nations began to return to the ideas and philosophies that were largely ignored during the Middle Ages. Without Rome to hold them together, the many different lands were forced to find their own identities. Men like Charlemagne and Otto I were able to unify many of the areas that had once been in the empire, but the full range of the Roman Empire was never again achieved, at least not from a governmental perspective.

The only unifying factor for Western Europe during the Middle Ages was the Christian Church, which became the Roman Catholic Church after the Great Schism. The religious figureheads continually consolidated power under the guise of religion until they had more power than nearly any monarch in Europe. The Church was jealous of any attempt to question that power and increasingly stifled thinking and science so that they would not lose their control over the continent.

The Italian Renaissance was the beginning of an entirely new era (called the early modern era). The leaders of the Renaissance typically did not directly challenge the Roman Catholic Church, but they were of the opinion that the Church should not have any say over the finding of truth in the world. Men like Galileo and Copernicus actually worked in the name of the Church, with Copernicus dedicating his masterwork, *On the Revolutions of the Heavenly Spheres*, to the Church. The Church repaid them by calling the work of the late Copernicus heretical and imprisoning Galileo. The more control the Church tried to exert over the people, the weaker it became.

As the Renaissance spread to the different nations in Europe, things began to change. Between the end of the 14th century and 1620, Europe emerged from the Middle Ages with a new understanding of their world.

Enabling the Renaissance

There were two things that had held the people of Europe back for much of the Middle Ages. The first was the difficulty with which food was produced. Even Rome had not really mastered a method of providing sustenance for the entire empire. Over the course of the Middle Ages, the tools and animals used to farm changed significantly. Harnesses were made that allowed for easier plowing of the fields, and new systems were implemented for planting and harvesting crops that made it easier to grow more food to feed more people. This allowed people to have more free time and to find other ways of making their lives simpler.

The second thing that held the people of the Middle Ages back was education. There were definitely people outside of the nobility and clergy who could read and write, but reading and writing were not common, even among some members of the nobility. Some clergy would teach people in their community how to read and write, particularly in the early days after the fall of Rome. Men, like King Alfred, also worked to educate people because they believed that was the best way to keep the people on the right path to salvation. Despite these good intentions, it was difficult to teach people because of the length of time it took to make a single book. Books had to be written by hand, which would usually take days or, in some cases, even weeks just to make a single book.

That all changed with Johannes Gutenberg and his printing press in the middle of the 15th century. For the first time in history, it was possible to mass produce books. Not only was it much easier to print a book, but it was also considerably cheaper to do because of the materials he used.

Without these innovations, the Renaissance would have been significantly different.

Attempting to Define Themselves

The term "Dark Ages" was actually coined as a way of defining the previous period of time as being less enlightened in terms of literature and thinking. It was a way of declaring that the men of the Renaissance were returning to the golden era of thinking that they thought occurred during the Roman Empire.

Architecture began to reflect the designs of the classical period instead of the impressive architectural style that developed during the Middle Ages. Buttresses and spires were abandoned for columns and marble. It gave the new buildings a more classical, clean, and sterile look that didn't require ornamentation. They did keep using the stained-glass windows though, proving that even the men of the Renaissance recognized the beauty of some of the architecture of the Middle Ages.

Instead of focusing on religion, men again turned their attention to mathematics and the sciences, which were neglected during the Middle Ages. The people who had fled from Constantinople after the fall of the Byzantine Empire were definitely instrumental in helping the people of Italy to understand and advance the ideas from the Roman period. Coupled with the innovations in these areas by the Muslims, the men of the Italian Renaissance had a huge platform from which to develop and evolve these fields. As mathematics and the sciences began to be explored in earnest, the people became energized and more inquisitive. This spirit of excitement soon traveled across the European continent.

Beyond Italy

The Renaissance started in Italy, but nearly every major nation enjoyed their own version of a renaissance, and no nation followed the same process or ideas as another. There was a booming interest in the amazing artwork and ideas that came out of Italy, but what the Renaissance meant for France and England was vastly different than what it was in Italy. Much of the focus in France was on aesthetics, particularly in art and architecture. Stunning buildings, such as the Palace of Versailles, were built during the French Renaissance, including the luxurious and impressive gardens. There was a rethinking of humanity and ethics, with writers like Moliere and Balzac being the most forward-thinking.

The English Renaissance reached its highest point under Queen Elizabeth I. She was the daughter of King Henry VIII and his second wife, Anne Boleyn, and under her guidance, the Renaissance had a somewhat different focus. Many of the works of William Shakespeare were written to entertain his audiences, but his histories focused on showing Elizabeth's ancestors in a positive light (even when that should not have been the case). There was a good bit of propaganda mixed in with the Renaissance, but this is understandable considering it was the only Protestant country in Europe. There were parts of the Holy Roman Empire that were Protestant, but each province had its own religion (there were many areas of the Holy Roman Empire that were Catholic).

Spain and Portugal saw similar types of renaissances that occurred in continental Europe, but they were more interested in pursuing their interests across the ocean in the Americas. Columbus reached the Americas 500 years after Leif Erikson but about 30 years before the Renaissance began. As most of Europe spent time reflecting and studying the world immediately around them, Spain and Portugal were exploring and exploiting the lands across the ocean. This left them with less time for the kind of soul searching and self-evaluation that occurred in other countries.

Flowing into the Present

The Renaissance was a surprisingly short period of about only a century or so. It is certainly true that there were some events that amplified the potential for changes that occurred during the Renaissance. Events like the Black Death served more as a bridge between the two time periods because Europe was already undergoing significant changes before the Renaissance. The Renaissance was just the first time that a large group of people began to progress the same ideas and values instead of each person or group working largely in a vacuum. The Middle Ages were focused on survival, establishing what was to come after Rome, and understanding their faith. All of that was fairly well defined by the time of the Renaissance. With these questions answered, and most of their necessities easily taken care of, the men of the Renaissance had the luxury of time to return to the ideas and philosophies of the Roman period.

Just like during the Middle Ages, pretty much any reason for a war served as a good enough reason to fight. By the start of the 17th century, the Protestant Reformation had sparked wars all across Europe. Despite the return to fighting, the ideologies and types of thinking that were prevalent during the Middle Ages were largely gone. Societies changed, with serfdoms largely disappearing. The Renaissance gave way to the Enlightenment Period, which saw significant advances in science, particularly physics. Inventions that changed the world came along with increasing frequency as well as regulations to those inventions, as it became clear that some were not entirely safe.

The people of the Middle Ages turned to the Christian god to solve their problems. After the Renaissance, they increasingly turned to science and research to resolve them instead. People began to decide that they wanted to be more in control of their lives instead of hoping for the best. This often resulted in findings that were just as horrific as they were astounding, but all of them were possible because of the shifts in thinking that started with the Renaissance.

Conclusion

There are many reasons why the years following the fall of Rome really were not a dark time and why the term Dark Ages really does a disservice to a period whose events helped shape the lands and future nations that made Europe into the way it is today. The most accurate interpretation of the term is that modern-day scholars and readers of history are kept in the dark about what happened during this time, as we don't know as much about this period compared to the Roman period or more recent history. A lot of the world was in chaos after Rome fell, but this was primarily among the ruling class and nobility, the people who would have been able to write records down for future generations. With the people who knew how to read and write becoming preoccupied with other problems and power struggles, the daily lives of the people and even some major events were completely lost to time.

One of the major changes that began during the Middle Ages was actually something that was not at all likely under Roman rule. Peasants and those who were born at the bottom of the social structure found that they had more options by the end of the Middle Ages. However, this was not the case during the time between when Rome fell and around 1000 CE. For instance, universities did not exist under the Roman Empire; those were a result of a move to equality (primarily for men, not women, though some of the clergy did teach girls and women). This was only possible after Rome fell because of the tight control the Romans had and how jealously they guarded influence and power.

The Dark Ages was a time when people began to expand their views and see more opportunities in the world around them. It was an incredibly slow process. Some of the leaders who rose during the Dark Ages forwarded education or focused on making the lives of the people in their domains better. Charlemagne and Alfred were among some of the most notable rulers who sought to implement better systems for their empires. As people experienced changes that brought them together with a larger group of people, they began to think in larger terms. The actions of the Vikings, for instance, taught the people of the continent that there were other ways to fight. The Vikings also began to expose how the Christian religion had become something that was completely different from what it was around the fall of Rome.

We do know some of the major events of this time and some key players, but we don't really know much more than that. Reading and writing were not common skills since people focused on survival and their religion (the changes to thinking were started, but a long way from fruition). Some of the greatest names that emerged from this time are still well known today, most notably Charlemagne. As Europe worked to redefine itself, the landscape frequently changed as people migrated and warred for territory. By the end of the Middle Ages, Europe had begun to transform into the nations of today. Some of them were fairly well defined, such as England, but some still had a long way to go, such as Austria and Germany. There was a spark of what was to come in all of them, though.

Check out more books by Captivating History

Bibliography

#203 Life of <u>Charlemagne</u>, 2019, Christian History Institute, christianhistoryinstitute.org

6 Reasons the Dark Ages Weren't So Dark, Sarah Pruitt, August 20, 2018, History, https://www.history.com

A Beginner's Guide to the Renaissance: Robert Wilde, April 15, 2018, ThoughtCo, www.thoughtco.com

A Brief History of the Vikings, Philip Parker and Tom Holland, History Extra, 2016, https://www.historyextra.com.

A Brief History of Venice, Italy, Tim Lambert, Local Histories, http://www.localhistories.org.

A Short History of the Caliphate: 632 AD – Present, History Hit, last updated February 19, 2019, https://www.historyhit.com.

Alfred the Great (849 AD – 899 AD), BBC: History, http://www.bbc.co.uk/history.

Alfred: King of Wessex, Dorothy Whitelock, Encyclopedia Britannica, last edited January 1, 2019, www.britannica.com.

Arianism, Encyclopedia Britannica, last edited October 9, 2015, www.britannica.com.

Battle of Tours, Tony Bunting, Encyclopedia Britannica, last edited March 28, 2017, www.britannica.com.

Byzantine Conference: Famous Emperors Famous Emperors, March 13, 2019, http://www.byzconf.org

Byzantine Empire: Historical Empire, Eurasia: John L. Terall, February 8 2019, Encyclopedia Britannica, www.britannica.com

Byzantine Empire: Mark Cartwright, September 19 2018, Ancient History Encyclopedia, www.ancient.eu/Byzantine_Empire/

Caliphate, Asma Afsaruddin, Encyclopedia Britannica, last edited January 18, 2019, www.britannica.com

<u>Charlemagne</u>, 2014, BBC, http://www.bbc.co.uk

Charlemagne's Reforms, Lumen Learning, https://courses.lumenlearning.com.

Christianity in the Roman Empire, Khan Academy, https://www.khanacademy.org.

Christmas, Hans J. Hillerbrand, Encyclopedia Britannica, last edited February 8, 2019, www.britannica.com.

Fall of Rome: How, When, Why Did It Happen, N.S. Gill, ThoughtCo, January 14, 2019, www.thoughtco.com/

Fall of Rome: How, When, Why Did It Happen, N.S. Gill, ThoughtCo, February 19, 2018, www.thoughtco.com/.

Fall of the western Roman Empire: Donald L. Wasson, April 12, 2018, Ancient History Encyclopedia Limited, www.ancient.eu

History: The Fall of Rome: Dr Peter Hether, February 17, 2011, BBC, www.bbc.co.uk

Holy Roman Emperor Otto I: Melissa Snell, February 16 2019, Though Co, www.thoughtco.com.

Leo III Attacked in a Procession, Dan Graves, 2019, JupiterImages Co, www.christianity.com

Lombards, Joshua J. Mark, December 6, 2014, Ancient History Encyclopedia, https://www.ancient.eu.

Louis I, John Contreni, Encyclopedia Britannica, last edited April 12, 2019, www.britannica.com.

Muslim Invasions of Western Europe: The 732 Battle of Tours, Kennedy Hickman, Limited, www.ancient.eu

Otto 1: Medieval Chronicles, 2014-2019, www.medievalchronicles.com.

Otto I: Encyclopedia of World Biography, 2004, The Gale Group Inc.

Petrarch: Italian Poet, John Humphreys Whitfield, Encyclopedia Britannica, last edited July 16, 2018, www.britannica.com.

Rise & Fall of the Roman, Ottoman & Byzantine Empires: Christopher Muscato, 2003-2019, study.com

Rurik and the Foundation of Rus', ER Services: Western Civilization, https://courses.lumenlearning.com/suny-hccc-worldhistory/.

Rurik Dynasty, Encyclopedia Britannica, last edited April 11, 2016, www.britannica.com.

Seal of the Prophets, Answering Islam, https://www.answering-islam.org/Index/index.html.

The Arian Controversy and the Council of Nicea, N. S. Gill, last edited May 22, 2019, Thought Co., https://www.thoughtco.com.

The Catholic Church, Lumen Learning, https://courses.lumenlearning.com.

The Lombards: A Germanic Tribe in Northern Italy, Melissa Snell, last edited March 15, 2018, Thought Co., https://www.thoughtco.com.

The Pagan Origins of Easter, Joanna Gillan, April 18, 2019, Ancient Origins, https://www.ancient-origins.net.

The Rise of Islamic Empires and States, Khan Academy, https://www.khanacademy.org.

The Spread of Islam, Oxford Islamic Studies Online, http://www.oxfordislamicstudies.com.

The Treaty of Verdun, Melissa Snell, ThoughtCo, October 21, 2018, www.thoughtco.com/.

Timeline of the Middle Ages, Simon Newman, *The Finer Times*.

Treaty of Verdun, Encyclopedia Britannica, last edited August 20, 2019, www.britannica.com.

Venice: History, Roberto Cessi and John Foot, Encyclopedia Britannica, www.britannica.com.

Vikings History: An Overview of the Culture and History of the Viking Age, Salem Media, History on the Net, last edited June 5, 2019, https://www.historyonthenet.com.

Who's Really the Last Roman Emperor?, Ken Lohatenpanot, August 17 2013, History Republic, historyrepublic.wordpress.com

World History 800-900 AD, History Central, https://www.historycentral.com.

www.ingramcontent.com/pod-product-compliance
Lightning Source LLC
LaVergne TN
LVHW040106080526
838202LV00045B/3795